Do You Remember When You Were Thirteen?

Tara came to Sunday school with gold glitter in her hair. Mike entered as a Don Johnson look-alike minus the stubble. Vickey wore a slinky dress obviously designed for an adult temptress. Pam came in with black fingernails and a black leather jacket over the modest dress her mother must have forced her to wear. Jani came in from sub-freezing weather in a lacy short-sleeve dress without a coat. Why? A coat would have covered the dress she obviously wanted to show off.

Parents and youth workers, don't despair. These children have not developed a sudden case of insanity; they are simply going through a stage. Like temper tantrums and teething, this, too, will pass.

But what do you do in the meantime?

Discover with Gary and Angela Hunt the keys to surviving the often outlandish, always confusing "tweenage" years. You'll find that life with a tween is not only survivable, but, at times, actually enjoyable.

"The Tweenage Years is a book filled with practical advice from two people who have counseled and loved young people for years. Parents, teachers, and youth workers will find a practical roadmap to help steer the children they love through these difficult years and into responsible adulthood."

> Jerry Falwell
> Pastor, Thomas Road Baptist Church

"This book is long overdue—a MUST for anyone who is a parent of junior highers or working with junior highers."

> Dave Adams
> Youth Pastor

SURVIVING THE TWEENAGE YEARS

A Guide for Parents and Youth Workers

By GARY & ANGELA HUNT

First Printing, February 1988

Published by
HERE'S LIFE PUBLISHERS, INC.
P. O. Box 1576
San Bernardino, CA 92402

Library of Congress Cataloging-in-Publication Data
Hunt, Gary.
Surviving the tweenage years.

1. Child rearing--United States. 2. Child rearing--
Religious aspects--Christianity. 3. Adolescent
psychology--United States. I. Hunt, Angela.
II. Title.
HQ769.H86   1988   649'.125   87-29329
ISBN 0-89840-205-0 (pbk.)

Scripture quotations are from the *King James Version* of
the Bible.

For More Information, Write:
L.I.F.E. – P.O. Box A399, Sydney South 2000, Australia
Campus Crusade for Christ of Canada – Box 300, Vancouver, B.C. V6C 2X3, Canada
Campus Crusade for Christ – Pearl Assurance House, 4 Temple Row, Birmingham, B2 5HG, England
Lay Institute for Evangelism – P.O. Box 8786, Auckland 3, New Zealand
Campus Crusade for Christ – P.O. Box 240, Colombo Court Post Office, Singapore 9117
Great Commission Movement of Nigeria – P.O. Box 500, Jos, Plateau State Nigeria, West Africa
Campus Crusade for Christ International – Arrowhead Springs, San Bernardino, CA 92414, U.S.A.

We lovingly dedicate this book to our parents

Ron and Jean Hunt
and
James and Frankie Elwell

who saw us through our own tweenage years.

Authors' Comments

We'd just like to say . . .

Most of the names mentioned in our stories have been changed. If there was a chance we'd cause embarrassment or any ill feeling from one of "our kids," we created a new name.

The English language can be awkward. Instead of referring constantly to "him or her" or "your son or daughter," we alternated between the sexes.

We owe a debt of gratitude to the kids who have let us enter their lives:

> To the tweenagers who are now grown and married, we're unbelievably proud of you!

> To those who are struggling through high school, remember we still love you. Give us a call sometime!

> To those who are still in our department, be patient with us. We'll be telling *your* stories next year!

Contents

A Time of Beginning and Expansion

Gary

Huntley was exasperated. I was driving him home from Sunday school, and as usual, was using the time to check up on how he was doing spiritually. Huntley had confessed that it was difficult to keep from cursing in school when his friends "cussed all the time."

"It's hard, Coach," he explained. "You gotta understand—I'm going through pooberty."

Angie and I had a good laugh over that one, but underlying Huntley's explanation was a solid fact: Going through puberty is not easy. Adolescence, strictly speaking, begins at puberty, but the rites of passage from childhood to adulthood begin when a child leaves elementary school and enters the neighborhood middle or junior high school.

It is in the middle school that a child becomes aware of older, more sophisticated preteens and teenagers. It is in the middle school that childhood toys are abandoned for record albums and designer clothes. It is the approach of middle school that leaves parents bewildered and confused.

I have pastored middle school students since 1975. While other pastors shudder at the thought of serving so long in such a position, I enjoy my work more each year. Parents who have sent two or three kids through our department will shake my hand and mutter, "I don't know how you do it."

How I do it is not as important as *why* I do it. I serve

middle school students because these in-between years are crucial. It is during this time that most kids go through their "ugly duckling" stage. When self-esteem is lowest, the pressures of life are greatest.

If you are a parent, teacher or a youth worker, I hope you will read this book with the pages of your memory open to the time when you were on the brink of maturity, poised for action but bereft of social skills, confidence and even the most basic physical coordination.

My own junior high years are vividly brought back every Sunday morning. When they enter our middle school Sunday school department as sixth graders, the boys have high voices, scrawny arms and legs, and scurry from classroom to bathroom in groups of three and four. The girls enter with a roll of baby fat, frilly dresses and a shy demeanor.

On promotion Sunday in June our new sixth graders sing loudly and lustily. It takes only a week or two for them to pick up on the self-conscious air which pervades the atmosphere, however, and soon our song leader once again will be pumping his arms like a crazed whooping crane, appreciating even a meager response from the crowd.

Ah, the sixth graders! They sit quietly, unobtrusively, in small groups of two and three. They are observant, obedient and dutiful. They learn Bible verses as easily as they learn their friends' phone numbers, and they enthusiastically join in games, quizzes and anything with hoopla.

The seventh graders are another category altogether. They have a year's experience in middle school to their credit, and they strut into the room like rowdy peacocks. The girls greet each other with loud squeals of approval, exclaim over each other's dresses, and reserve long rows of chairs for their groups of friends. During the

10

singing they shyly whisper the words of the songs as they look to their friends for support and shared giggles.

The boys wait outside the door until their buddies have arrived, then they enter with a rush of energy. Seventh grade boys fidget during the singing and fidget during the lesson. They make paper airplanes out of handouts and slyly try to annoy the "uncool" kids in the front of the room by flinging spitballs or paperwads.

What a transformation occurs between the seventh and eighth grades. Sudden sophistication! Overnight cool! Somehow, magically over the summer, the eighth grade girls seem to grow within an inch of their adult height. They wear clothing that would rival any career woman's wardrobe; they carry handbags to match their Sunday pumps. Makeup is applied carefully and colorfully; their hair is curled, coiffed, and firmly set in place with mousse, setting gel or hairspray—whatever happens to be the element of choice that season.

These "matrons" of our middle school department glide into the room with ease and confidence. They greet their friends with a slow smile, turn once or twice to discreetly display their outfits, and after checking with a friend to see which row of chairs has been appropriately reserved, seek out their seats with all the confidence of a titled lady approaching the royal box. Confidence, grace, and a certain upper-class attitude simply ooze from them.

During the class, these girls sit quietly, only occasionally taking glances at the section of chairs occupied by the eighth grade boys. These boys haven't made as drastic a change as the girls, but they, too, are aware of their new-found influence as eighth graders. Their hair is cut just-so; their outfits carefully chosen to exhibit either an air of Sunday dash or Saturday flash. Few of the eighth graders sing. Even fewer have the inclination to learn memory verses.

What has happened to those sweet little sixth graders who were reluctant to retire their Cabbage Patch dolls from active duty? Regardless of whether or not physical puberty has arrived, the middle school mentality has led them from childhood to adolescence, from an end to a beginning. As adolescence is the bridge between childhood and adulthood, so the middle school years are the bridge between childhood and adolescence.

Middle school students, ages ten to thirteen, are not children but not yet fully teenagers. These "tweenagers" have unique needs, and you will find special considerations helpful as you parent or work with them. This is a rewarding area of ministry, an invisible investment which can lay a firm foundation for the times of testing and temptation ahead. Come with us as we explore and enjoy this much-ignored "tweenage."

1

Tweenagers in a Word? Extreme!

Angie

All adolescents are, in a sense, psychotic.
— Fanita English

Tara came to Sunday school with gold glitter in her hair. Mike entered as a Don Johnson look-alike minus the stubble. Vickey wore a slinky dress obviously designed for an adult temptress. Pam came in with black fingernails and a black leather jacket over the modest dress her mother must have forced her to wear. Jani came in from sub-freezing weather in a lacy short-sleeve dress without a coat. I knew the reason instinctively: A coat would have covered the dress she obviously wanted to show off.

Parents, don't despair. These children have not developed a sudden case of insanity; they are simply going through a stage. Like a temper tantrums and teething, this, too, will pass. Tweenagers react against the symbols of both childhood and adulthood. They form their own bizarre sub-culture with extremes in every area: Their clothing is of the wildest color and style; their music contains the heaviest beat and most outlandish acts; their heroes are wildly worshipped; and their peer group is the most set in its conformity.

I remember a cartoon I read sometime during the 1970s. A bearded, long-haired, blue-jeaned peacenik stood before his father and pleaded: "But Dad, I've *got* to be a non-conformist. How else can I be like everybody else?"

Erase the beard and change the long hair to what today's fashions are and you have the perfect picture of a tweenager. "But Mom and Dad," we hear kids saying, "we've got to be different from you. How else can we be like kids?"

Should you let your son have pink hair? Should you let your daughter listen to heavy metal rock groups which bite off the heads of rats in performances? Should you let your daughter *or* son have three pierced holes in her or his ears?

Gauge each behavior by biblical standards. If the behavior is not a cultural symbol of rebellion and if it can be done and God still glorified, then let your tween express himself or herself.

Be prepared for anything — the tweenage years are the age of the *extreme*.

Extreme Hero Worship

I'll never forget one Sunday morning a couple of years ago. We had a musical team from our local college in to do a presentation, and one of their skits included a reference to Michael Jackson, who was then at the peak of his popularity.

Several of our "bus kids" were seated down front.

14

These were nice kids who came on the church bus every Sunday and rarely gave us a moment's trouble. True, they never seemed to pay much attention and we couldn't see why they bothered to come at all since they roamed the halls much of the time, but they came without fail and always chose front-row, center seats.

When one of the performing college students broke out in a portrayal of Michael Jackson (complete with white glove), a hornet's nest broke loose in the front section. One girl stood up, exclaiming loudly, "Michael doesn't look anything like that!" Another yelled, "Don't you act like that!"

When the startled college student started to speak, he was cut off by still another girl, "You hush up!" Jackson's loyal fans stood up and huffed out of the room, all because an unfortunate worker attempted to take the name of Michael Jackson in vain.

Strong hero worship is a trait of tweenagers, and it can be used in the ministry and in parenting if the young person is presented with heroes worthy of emulation.

One Sunday morning we had a guest teacher who asked the 300 middle schoolers in our class for a response to his question: "Who are your heroes?" When no one answered, he ventured out into the rows of kids, calling on students individually.

"Who is your hero?" he asked one student.

"Dr. J," the boy replied.

"Who is your hero?" he asked a girl.

"Princess Diana."

"Who is your hero?" he asked another boy.

The boy paused a moment and thought. "I guess Gary Hunt is," he answered. Imagine! The boy chose his youth pastor for a hero!

Any youth pastor or senior pastor should be worthy

15

of the hero worship from those he leads. Not only does a pastor or leader represent spiritual authority, but he is also a friend, a counselor, an advisor, a teacher and a helper. In many situations he may also be a substitute parental figure. Even kids from "good" homes will look for what psychologists call "the significant other," a person outside the family circle who provides leadership and affirmation.

Extreme Avoidance of Parents

Many parents are jealous of the affection their children lavish upon youth workers, teachers or older friends. They feel overlooked and unappreciated. Parents are often deeply hurt when their kids obviously prefer the company of some new and more exciting adult.

Parents, your child has not outgrown his need for you—it is the adult/baby role he has outgrown. He's embarrassed to be seen in public with you. He'd rather drop into a bottomless pit than let his friends see him "helping mommy" or "having daddy with him to shop for clothes." When you drop your tween off at the neighborhood arcade for an afternoon with friends, don't be surprised if he asks to be let out at the far corner. *He is simply embarrassed to be seen having his parents do something for him which he cannot yet do for himself.*

I remember well my own junior high days. I was involved in the science program and the concert choir, and whenever concert contests or science fairs came around, I rejoiced that I could travel for a day or two and be independent and away from my parents. It wasn't that I disliked or didn't respect them—it was simply great to be on my own: ordering what I wanted in restaurants, checking into a hotel with *my* friends (and a chaperon lurking around the corner), participating in an endeavor that was my responsibility alone. If my parents were able to drive and meet me at the site, I doubt that I even *spoke* to them until

16

I reluctantly rejoined them back at school when the event was over. I was glad that they cared enough to come and see me perform, but I simply preferred to mix, mingle, and be seen on my own or with my friends.

Heartless? Now I think so, but then I felt independent and — well — sophisticated. In the eighth grade, you see, I knew everything.

This desire to be independent is natural and provides the foundation for the independence you will want your child to have in later years. Some children are more independent than others (particularly first-born children), and this desire for independence manifests itself at different times for each child.

Becky and Sarah, two tweenage sisters, went off to church camp for one week. Becky, the oldest girl, loved every minute and was disgruntled to return home. Sarah, who had not been able to join in the camp activities with the same enthusiasm as Becky, cried herself to sleep every night from homesickness and was thrilled to be back with mom and dad.

Their mother admitted that Sarah's homesickness was flattering. "I was relieved that Sarah missed us and annoyed that Becky didn't," she said.

But the girls' father understood his daughters' behaviors: "Becky is more responsible and more ready to be independent," he said. "She has had more opportunities to grow up and is closer to being the strong Christian woman we'd like her to be someday. It isn't bad that Sarah was homesick, but we need to realize that the girls are far apart in social development."

As the invisible umbilical cord between parents and children stretches thin, tweenagers begin to form other relationships. They establish their places in a peer group, reach out for new adult influences and begin to open themselves to a host of friendships. Although during the tweenage years children see the world as *us* (tweenagers) against *them* (adults), one or two significant influences are allowed to penetrate the peer group.

Extreme Crushes

As tweenagers seek new adult influences, boys and girls sometimes develop passionate emotional attachments to older women and men. Though boys do not often develop a crush on an older woman (and when they do, rarely do they do anything about it other than daydream), most girls go through at least one mad crush on an older male figure.

My husband and I have noticed that girls who have no father in the home or who have an "absentee" father are especially prone to develop a crush on a youth leader. Personally, I'd much rather have my daughter develop a crush on her youth pastor than on the latest rock singer, but parents who are concerned about these "affairs of the heart" can be assured that they are harmless unless unnaturally encouraged.

We have an old bureau in our garage in which we store odds and ends and bits and pieces of our lives. The bottom drawer is crammed full of cards, sentimental letters and notes from tweenagers of years past. Those notes, handwritten and invariably folded into tiny football shapes or intricate self-envelopes, always remind us of just how passionate and innocent is that first case of hero worship. Here are a couple from our collection:

Gary:

I'm not mad, just upset. I feel like you don't care about me. I know you do but you hardly ever spend any time with me. I love you and I want you to love me back. I know you do, I think, and if you do you don't show it very much.

Dear Gary:

    I love you very, very, very, very much. How have you been doing? Have you ever gotten mad or upset at me? Why? Please tell me. It would mean a lot to me. Have I ever hurt your feelings? If I have ever, forgive me because I am sorry! How have you been doing mentally, physically, spiritually? I'm sorry that I don't have any fancy writing paper. Well I just wanted to say "hi" and I love you! Keep on praying for me!

These may sound like ardent love letters, and in a sense they are. But these girls are just learning about the rush of feeling that "love" brings, and they are in love with the emotion more than anything else. Furthermore, their definition of "love" does not contain the element of sexuality that is inherent in an adult relationship.

Help Your Tween Through "First Love"

What do you do if your tweenage daughter develops a severe crush on an older or inappropriate male figure? First, talk to her and find out exactly who this person is. Try not to assume the role of an interrogator or make quick, harsh judgments about the object of your child's affection. Simply listen and try to understand. If you laugh, fuss or decide to ignore the state of affairs, your daughter will reason, "My parents simply don't understand. Why did I ever think they could?" Do not forbid the feelings—your child will simply say, "I can't control my emotions!" Then her feelings will not only be passionate, but desperately passionate.

After you know with whom your daughter is infatuated, judge whether this person can be trusted around your adoring daughter. If he is a responsible adult, don't worry, but continue to be cautious. If he is an adult with whom you are not acquainted, get to know him. Go for a visit and say, "My daughter thinks a lot of you and I wanted

19

to meet you." If he is aware that your daughter has a crush on him, he will wisely continue to be nice, but not too encouraging or harsh.

Make sure your child isn't spending unreasonable amounts of time with this person, and try to make sure they are not spending unsupervised time alone. Never assume anyone is totally harmless. Even youth pastors and teachers who may need to privately counsel your daughter should have other people around.

But if the crush amounts to nothing but "sighing" from afar, let it go. Scores of girls have had crushes on my husband, and we've seen their feelings grow from first love to a fatherly appreciation. He has performed the wedding ceremonies of many of those girls, and now they have established homes of their own.

Extreme Activity

All tweenagers, boys and girls, gravitate to adults who are exciting and fun. Those who work with tweenagers should recognize this and make sure activities planned for this age group are fast-paced, colorful and well-planned. If you are planning a party for your tweenage kid, you can't go wrong if you make food your highest priority. The best food? Pizza! It is fast, filling and self-serve; just be sure there is plenty of it. I've seen one junior high boy eat an entire large pizza in fifteen minutes.

Our senior high school department annually sponsors a Hawaiian luau. They painstakingly plan decorations, costumes, games and an elaborate menu. The outdoor site of the luau takes a week to prepare; the food is cooked days ahead; and special music and lots of little "extras" are provided—a souvenir program, leis for all who attend, background Hawaiian music during the dinner itself.

All of the above would be wasted on junior highers.

Tweenagers give only a cursory glance to decorations; the programs would inevitably be folded into paper airplanes; the boys would refuse to wear flowers; and the Hawaiian music would be drowned out during dinner by belching and scuffling. The best activity for tweenagers is something fast and physical. Take your tweenagers skating, feed them pizza, and you'll be a hero.

Extreme Humor

Many adults would be slightly sickened by the sight of a room in which tweenagers have just eaten. *Any* adult would be nauseated by a full dose of the gastronomical humor which comes naturally to teenage boys. Teenage humor, to the adult mind, is perverted.

This is the age of "boogie humor," when bodily functions are outrageously funny and food is not only meant to be eaten but chewed, played with, displayed, barfed and re-eaten. To the young adolescent mind, the grossest jokes (or sights or sounds) are the funniest.

There are times when *everything* is funny to a tweenager. Thomas Cottle, writing in *12 to 16,* remembers his own early adolescent years:

> We laughed at styles of appearance and voice, and, best of all, tangible deformity drove us into hysterics. Knowing it was dreadful of us, we nonetheless could rarely contain ourselves if we caught a buddy's eyes in class or while riding a bus. Someone would be overly fat, or tall, or dressed differently, or have long hair, or slip on a stair, or ask a bus driver in "broken" English for the location of a street, and we would look and listen intently and then, blam, we would be busting with the pains of laughter, the tears rolling down our cheeks, and grappling to catch some inner strand or throw a switch that might bring us back to normalcy.[1]

Extreme Manners – The Verbal Jest

Tweenagers are masters of the "put-down" – particularly if the cut is on someone else. While a tweenager's self-esteem is usually incredibly fragile, he enjoys nothing more than hearing his best friend or youth leader cut to ribbons. My husband has a bald spot on the top of his head and a sure way for another worker to win the "respect" of our kids is to make a cutting remark about Gary's bald spot.

Tweenagers love to hear sarcastic humor because they are tremendously self-conscious. They are awkward and insecure and, more than anything, they fear public embarrassment. When a youth pastor or worker gets a public cut, they laugh along in relief and devilish joy that someone else is on the hot seat for the moment.

Youth workers, however, use the put-down on kids at their own risk. Calling a kid "chicken lips" in public may win a laugh, but it may also alienate that kid forever. Youth workers should be sure that the kid who is an object of a joke has enough self-assurance to handle the public attention and knows that no harm is intended.

There are always some kids who are upset when the youth pastor or worker *doesn't* tease them – they feel left out of the camaraderie. But keep in mind that tweenagers are hypersensitive and what may be a joke to you can be a serious blow to an insecure young person.

Parents, a word of advice: Don't use the put-down with your kids (or with each other). "Gosh," one girl told me after I counseled her about her low self-image, "even my mother says I'm a klutz." The mother may have been playfully joking, but the words remained in her daughter's mind. *If your parents don't stick up for you,* kids reason, *who will?*

Put-Downs in Anger

Often tweenagers let loose with a string of put-downs more in anger than in jest. They are using the put-down as self-defense, a form of verbal fighting which often leads to physical aggression. Virtually every fist fight between boys starts with a verbal insult.

How do we help tweenagers keep a guard on their tongues? First, *we* must make the resolution never to put down a child in anger. Our speech needs to be positive. As parents, when our children need rebuking, never criticize the child—correct the action.

"You are stupid, lazy and dumb!" shouted Joe's father. "We do everything for you and you don't have the gratitude to do a simple thing like taking out the garbage when we asked you to!"

A wiser father would have said, "Son, because you went off without putting the garbage out, your mother and I were late for an important appointment. Your action was thoughtless. I know you can do better."

Young teenagers need praise and affirmation, not criticism or condemnation. By controlling our own tongues and emphasizing the biblical teaching on the tongue (James 1:26; 3:1-12; and the book of Proverbs), we can teach our children to cultivate wholesome, productive speech.

Extreme Energy

You may have noticed that tweens often have trouble controlling their bodies. Aside from the awkwardness which accompanies rapid growth, Edward Martin, who taught junior high students for several years, noticed a "general twitchiness" among his students. "Movement was the standard," he relates, "tapping of hands or fingers, wiggling bodies, turning heads, bouncing, jiggling, squirming. These were not the exuberant and free movements of small children, nor the coordinated and powerful movements of youth, but rather an uncontrolled display and use of body."[2]

Extreme – But Fleeting – Commitments

Martin also noticed the instant and complete commitment of tweenagers to a person, idea, activity or event:

> Four months after I had stopped teaching a particular group of seventh grade students, I appeared in the school lunch room where many from the class were eating. A cry went up "There's Mr. Martin!" and suddenly I was surrounded by eight bubbling girls and boys all talking at once, all asking a string of questions about where I was and what I was doing. By the time I had recovered from the charge and my ego had hopelessly swelled, I realized I was alone again. The eight had returned to their other activities just as fast as they had come.[3]

Are you ready for the extreme world of the tweenager?

2

Preparing For Adolescence

Angie

---

*My mother had a great deal of trouble with me,
but I think she enjoyed it.*
—Mark Twain

Mary and Jason are alarmed. They have worked in the youth department as volunteers for five years, but now *their* son is in junior high and the changes in him have caught them off guard.

"If only I had known this was coming!" wailed Mary one afternoon. "I thought I was prepared, but I never dreamed adolescence would be like this! My son is a different child!"

Don't Dread Adolescence

My high school English teacher gave me the key to

writing a good expository theme: "Tell 'em what you're gonna tell 'em, then tell 'em, then tell 'em what you told 'em." If you want to peacefully survive the "tweenage years," first learn what's going to happen, then watch it happen, then reflect (and rejoice!) on what happened. It's a natural process and one you can learn from. These years may be difficult, but, to quote the old mountain climber, it's the *bumps* in life you climb on!

What can parents do to prepare themselves and their children for the onset of the tweenage years?

First, don't dread the adolescent years. They are natural, normal, and can be fun and exciting! You are not losing your dutiful son or daughter—you are gaining a young person on the road to independence! You are beginning the most crucial building program you have ever undertaken.

What man plans to build a lovely home and then dreads the actual building process? Suppose a couple plans to build their dream home. For years they carefully save every extra dollar and search through house plans and pictures. When they are financially able, they choose exactly the right lot after months of careful surveying. After weeks of further planning, they hire a contractor, finalize their house plans and arrange a date for the foundation to be poured.

This couple knows the actual building process may take two or three months, but their lovely home will be worth the wait. Why should they be nervous about beginning to build? Building can be fun! They have planned well, and they trust their builder. There is no reason why their home will not be a success.

Seeing a child through adolescence is not much different. If you plan for the tweenage years and trust the Master Builder, the finished creation will be a glorious success. There is no need to fear the years ahead.

So what's the plan?

Communicate With Respect and Consideration

The Smiths and their son, Jonathan, were driving home from church. "What was your lesson about today, Jon?" drilled his mother.

Jon felt like he was under examination. He was dismally reminded of a harsh teacher at school, but he quietly mumbled, "Nothing much."

"Nothing?" queried his father. "You didn't get anything out of the lesson? Didn't you listen?"

"Yes, I listened!" snapped Jon. "It was just the old story about Daniel and the lions' den. I've heard it a million times."

"I tell you, Dear," said Mr. Smith to Mrs. Smith, "these kids aren't learning anything. Someone isn't doing his job. Perhaps I should speak to the pastor about Jon's Sunday school teacher."

Meanwhile, the Johnsons were driving home with their son, Tim. "Did you enjoy the lesson today, Tim?" asked his mother.

"Yeah, it was OK," replied Tim. "The story of Daniel and the lions' den."

"That was always my favorite story," remarked Mr. Johnson. "I always thought if I could have half as much courage as Daniel, I'd do OK in the world."

"What do you think, Tim?" asked Mrs. Johnson. "Would you like to be as courageous as Daniel?"

"You bet. Maybe then I'd have the guts to tell the guys in my science class to stop giving the teacher a hard time. I could do a lot of things if I had that kind of courage."

"Well, Tim," his mother replied, "What's to stop

27

you from having Daniel's courage? You know the same God."

Instead of verbally attacking your tweenager like the Smiths, encourage creative responses. Talk to your child with the same good manners and consideration you'd give another adult.

When your child was younger, the adult/child role was appropriate. Now, however, your child is assuming his own independence, and you should not continue to talk to him like a child.

Some of the most effective children's workers I know are people who simply acknowledge that children exist. When you meet a couple with their little children in tow, do you take the time to greet the children after you've greeted their parents? Do you talk about your children's personal problems when your children are standing nearby, as if they can't hear you? Children, even tweenagers, are accustomed to being "talked down to" or ignored by adults.

Talk to your children as loving leaders, not as drill sergeants. You'll find that a little respect goes a long way.

Involve Your Child in Creative Thinking

When you need to discipline your child, ask for his input. "What do you think it would take for you to learn this lesson?" a parent could ask.

When your daughter comes home from school and tells you that Mary and Susie are fighting because Mary misunderstood what Susie meant when she said Stephanie liked Jeff more than Mary, ask your daughter what could have been done to ease the situation without fighting and anger. Encourage your tween to express her ideas and opinions.

Get to Know the Adults in Your Child's Life

Historically, young teenagers were quickly assigned to apprenticeships where older and wiser adults guided them through the transition from childhood to maturity. This adult relationship provided the bridge upon which the child passed into responsible adulthood. Sadly, even though young people are crying out for adults to emulate, there are few adults today who have the time or inclination to invest their lives in young people. Seeking that outside influence, tweenagers often find that the peer group is their only bridge to adulthood. The peer group does not offer the wisdom, experience, responsibility or knowledge young people need, but it does offer acceptance.

If your child is fortunate during his tweenage years, he will be able to establish friendships with adults apart from you, his parents. Up until this time his adult acquaintances have been your friends, but during the tweenage years children begin to seek out individual adult relationships. These friendships may be established with favorite teachers or coaches, youth pastors, a neighbor or a Scout master. Not all of these relationships will be beneficial; some may even be dangerous. Get to know, at least on an informal basis, the other adults with whom your child interacts.

The youth workers in your church have a special job—to oversee the spiritual life of your child during these crucial years. Take the time to meet and talk with your child's youth pastor or Sunday school teacher. There may be a time when he or she will need your input or help.

A good youth worker supports parents, recognizes that all families are different, and keeps the lines of communication open between parents, tweenagers and the church.

Expect a Change of Identity

In sixth grade I was known as Angela Elwell. I wore my hair short, pulled tightly with a barrette to one side of my head. I had buck teeth and was the only one in my class who still wore anklet socks with my tennis shoes. I made straight *A's* and favored the library over outdoor activities. My teachers were my best friends.

In the seventh grade I decided to change myself. I began calling myself "Angie" and writing my "t's" the old-fashioned way, without a crossbar and with the upward swoop at the end of a word. I found two other best friends; we became a threesome. I loosened up — gone were the ankle socks and the barrette, and my grades began to include some *B's*. Braces took care of the buck teeth. I stopped wearing my cousin's hand-me-downs and began to sew some of my own clothes. Friends, and acceptance, had become more important than the library and my teachers.

Today I still cross my "t's" the old-fashioned way, and my close friends still call me Angie. The changes I consciously made in the seventh grade have, for the most part, remained.

Your child, too, will probably change some part of his identity. He will shuck off the identity you have given him as easily as he discards the clothes you buy him. Some of these passing phases will be incorporated into the person he will ultimately become; others will fade away. I went through an "I-am-an-animal-lover" phase and my mother had to cope with breeding gerbils, two baby chicks, kittens, a dog, a parakeet, and my intense desire for baby rabbits. (Only the dog and a parakeet are in my household today.) Tweenagers simply "try on" different identities to see which ones suit them best.

Along with this search for identity comes the accompanying fear that the person inside will not measure up to the accepted standard. Each tweenager wrestles with two sets of characteristics: an unchangeable physical set (hair and eye color, body size, facial features) and a much larger, intangible set which can only be defined by comparison with his peers. Jerome Kagan says the latter set "includes adjectives like intelligent, wise, athletic, brave, pretty, confident, independent, responsible, and sociable. Assignment to positions on these dimensions, by adult or child, requires the slippery judgement of comparison."[1]

Help Your Child Discover Who He Is

Tweenagers are labeled by peers, family, church workers, teachers and even physicians. Often labels are applied too soon, and a child never realizes that he or she could outgrow or outperform a negative label.

Labels have surprising staying power. I remember Donald Shockey, who was labeled our class "brain" in the sixth grade. Donald lived up to his name, ultimately graduating near the top of our high school class. (Everyone was amazed when someone else turned out to be valedictorian.) And though Donald was good-looking, no one ever considered him a "hunk" because he was the "brain."

When I took my first teaching job I replaced a teacher who had left two weeks into the school year. My students were unknown to me, and I graded their first essays with a strict and impartial eye. When I handed Andrea's paper back to her, she turned pale and I thought she might faint. You see, Andrea was the brain of her class and no teacher had ever given her less than a 95. I had given her essay a 93! She spent an hour after class with me, thoroughly probing my grading system so she would never fall short again.

How can you help a tweenager as he begins to discover his own identity? Bruce B. Barton has outlined several suggestions:

1. Prevent premature closure. Avoid using labels such as "You're no good at math," "You're great in sports," or "You'll probably be a preacher." We have to keep reminding our children that they are worth infinitely more to God than any evaluation parents or friends pin on them.

2. Expose tweens to various constructive and healthy adult role models. Perhaps they can work at a summer camp or get a job with a relative.

3. Remember to show joy and pleasure in your life, your work, and in your adult sexuality. Don't allow your tween to believe that people die emotionally when they reach age twenty-one.

4. Help kids arrange priorities for their capabilities. Some children have more than one interest or ability. A child may like softball, biology, church work and computers. That doesn't mean he has to be a Christian, softball-playing, computer-biologist. It is possible to develop some abilities as hobbies and still others as occasional interests.

5. Grant recognition by giving honest approval for the things they do well. Help them to recognize and see their strengths in skills, knowledge and attitudes.

6. Screen your own expectations of them. Make sure you are not prompting them toward something that is out of their depth.

7. Reassure them and yourself that adolescence does involve some suffering.

8. Talk about your Christianity. Describe your own life experiences that have brought you to your conclusions. Use the principle of pointing rather than telling. Give your tween the opportunity to draw his own conclusions and to challenge and

disagree with you. Urge him to back up what he says.

9. Above all, make sure that during this time period you build up their identity in Christ rather than their identity based on how well they perform. So many people judge other persons on appearance or performance rather than as human beings loved and created by God.[2]

I used to have a youth pastor who made each of us memorize this slogan:

I!

I am!

I am me!

I am me and I am good!

I am me and I am good because God don't make no junk!

It seems silly now, but whenever things were rough growing up or whenever I had been hurt by another person, I used to mumble under my breath, "I! I am! I am me! I am me and I am good! . . ." Believe me—it worked!

Teach your tweenagers something they can fall back on when times get rough. As parents, assure them that the love you feel for them goes beyond "I love you because you're my kid." Specify and name positive character attributes that you love and appreciate in your child. You'll help him discover who he really is.

If you work with young people, be willing to be the significant adult friend in a tweenager's life. With your friendship for support, strong loving parents, and the knowledge that God loves them deeply and personally, tweenagers will be well on their way to finding a wholesome identity.

Respect Your Child's Desire for Privacy

It is during the tweenage years that your child's bedroom door will be closed for hours on end. "What is she doing in there?" a parent may wonder. Don't worry. Your daughter may be reading, dreaming, writing, gazing into the mirror or examining her rapidly-changing body. Allow her time for introspection.

Your tweenager may be an introvert. Forcing her to participate in group activities when she is unsure of herself will only accentuate the differences between her shyness and the boisterous attitude of others. Give your child room to find herself.

Don't Withhold Physical Affection

Although your child may pull away in embarrassment and may blush, keep giving those hugs of approval and affection. Just don't do it in front of "the guys."

Let your child set the boundaries for physical contact. A self-conscious tween will not be as eager to receive those hugs and kisses as the seven-year-old you once knew, but it's not necessary to avoid all physical affection. Respect your child's limits, all the while assuring him of your faithful support and love.

Give Your Child the Freedom to Make Decisions

A college student I recently counseled moaned, "I've never had a job and I've never had a budget. I'd like to get out of school but I have no place to go but home, no money, and no skills. I wouldn't even know how to begin to balance a checkbook."

This young woman is unfortunate. Her parents never gave her the opportunity or the responsibility of providing anything for herself. Everything she needed was given to her; she was accountable for nothing.

You can begin to develop your child's autonomy in late elementary school. You might begin by allowing your child to choose his own school clothes within a certain budget. Soon you might give him an allowance for school supplies and teach him how to spend wisely on the things he will need.

When children enter early adolescence, they should be able to responsibly handle minor decisions regarding their friends, music, activities, wardrobe, schoolwork and hobbies. Give them the freedom to decide for themselves while you are there to help them.

Keep Your Marriage Strong

Adolescence is difficult enough without battling the grief and guilt of a broken home. No matter how amicable a divorce may be, psychologists have noted that nearly all children see themselves as the reason for the breakup of the family.

Take the time to keep your marriage strong. Spend quiet time alone with your spouse and recapture the romance of your marriage. Show by example how a Christian man and woman conduct themselves lovingly and respectfully in a marriage ordained by God. Your example may be the best reason your child will have for maintaining high moral standards when she begins to date and to seek a life's partner.

Take a few moments to talk with your tweenager about marriage. By casually asking "What sort of person do you want to marry?" and continuing the discussion, you can begin to instill the values your daughter or son will need for a solid foundation when they begin to seriously consider marriage.

Have Fun as a Family

"Family Together Night" is an idea whose time has come. In a day when fathers and mothers work and children are busier than ever with school activities, families often fracture into individuals with separate agendas.

Set aside one night for the family. Keep the calendar clear of all other events, including church, television, work and school commitments. Search through idea books for fun activities and educational ventures that will be entertaining for the entire family. If the age span of your children is broad, have the children take turns selecting an activity for the family. A family is a team, and no team can expect to be successful without practice, communication and an exuberant team spirit.

Lead Your Child to Christ at an Early Age

Children of seven and eight are able to understand spiritual conditions and make a commitment to their faith. Statistics indicate that relatively few people make a commitment to Christ after age twelve, and the odds against a salvation decision grow greater with each passing year.

When I interviewed Dr. Clyde Narramore, the pioneer in the field of Christian psychology, he advised me on one of the best ways parents can show love to their children:

> Lead a child to the Lord at an early age and then help him to walk each day with God. Help him understand that God is the Creator of all things. Lead him in paths of righteousness. Explain everything in spiritual terms as much as possible. Say, "Look at that tree. It's continually pumping water to its many parts. There's a wonderful pumping system inside the tree. Do

you know who put it there? The Lord did."

Really, it doesn't take an awful lot of maturity to realize that you've done things that are wrong, that sin displeases God, and that God sent Jesus Christ to die for us. Children can use computers at three and four. They can know and do much by the time they are five. Consequently, they can understand the gospel at a very young age.

I think it may be detrimental to a person's intellect if he has to live in this world and not understand many basic facts such as sin, salvation, Christian growth and God's working throughout the world.[3]

Don't let your tweenagers go through the adolescent years spiritually unprepared. Rich spiritual knowledge can give your child wisdom beyond his years and see him through many difficult situations.

Making the Transition

The best preparation for the tweenage years and the launch of adolescence is a good parent/child relationship which has been nurtured throughout the childhood years. If you love your child and maintain open and honest communication, and if you place a strong emphasis on spiritual growth and development, your entrance into the tweenage years will be smoother.

3

Tweens
Under Peer Pressure

Gary

Don't laugh at a youth for his affectations;
he's only trying on one face after another
till he finds his own.
—*Logan Pearsall Smith*

James Dobson, writing in *Parents and Teenagers*,
reports the following:

> Dr. Urie Bronfenbrenner, eminent authority
> on child development at Cornell University, told
> a Senate committee that the junior high years
> are probably the most critical to the development
> of a child's mental health. It is during this period
> of self-doubt that the personality is often as-
> saulted and damaged beyond repair. Conse-
> quently, said Bronfenbrenner, it is not unusual
> for healthy, happy children to enter junior high

school, but then emerge two years later as broken, discouraged teenagers.

I couldn't agree more emphatically with Bronfenbrenner's opinion at this point. Junior high school students are typically brutal to one another, attacking and slashing a weak victim in much the same way a pack of northern wolves kill and devour a deformed carabao. Few events stir my righteous indignation more than seeing a vulnerable child—fresh from the hand of the Creator in the morning of his life—being taught to hate himself and despise his physical body and wish he had never been born.[1]

Tweenagers are the most insecure people in the world. The thing they ardently seek is often the most difficult and fleeting goal to pursue: status and approval from their peers.

What gives status? James S. Coleman studied 7,000 students in Illinois in 1957, and his findings are still valid today. Having high grades is not a basis for popularity among tweens, but being an athlete, being in the "leading crowd," and being a leader in activities are important to boys. Being in the leading crowd, being a leader in activities, and having nice clothes are most important to girls.[2]

This is the age of group conformity, and, fortunately, there are always several groups into which a tweenager may fit. Unfortunately, not all groups are accepted or given the "seal of approval." In our middle school department at church we have clearly defined cliques. There is a group of wealthy girls who dress like career women, a group of physically immature giggly girls, a punk group, a spiritual group, an athletic group, an apathetic group, a group of the juvenile delinquents of tomorrow, an in-between group, and a group of social misfits. This last group, made up of

40

tweens who act "different," dress "different" or come from "weird" families, comes in each Sunday and sits together although the kids never exchange a word. Even in their solitary state as outcasts, they find each other. It is difficult to be different at this time of life when it is so important to be like others.

Insensitive Peer Groups

As Dobson mentioned, tweenagers can be the most unfeeling creatures in the world. Many school teachers can testify that students who are "outcasts" miss a lot of school because they so dread meeting their enemies that they become physically ill. I have seen a group of tweenagers taunt another girl or boy until the victim ran crying to an adult for help. Why do the groups tease so unmercifully? Their aggressiveness is a sort of *unity*. They enjoy the confrontation and treading the dangerous line between tolerance and direct adult intervention.

We were on a week-long choir trip when I noticed a situation developing between Sarah and Christopher. Sarah was a leader in a group of pretty, well-dressed, popular girls. Christopher was a quiet, brainy, sensitive loner. Sarah and her group were passing the hours by teasing thirteen-year-old Christopher. Sarah would sit by him on the bus, lean over and say sweetly, "I love you, Christopher."

Christopher was always reduced to a blushing mass of insecurity and Sarah would quickly retreat while her friends dissolved into giggles. This teasing continued over several days and we were at a loss. How could we stop Sarah without making Christopher feel defenseless against a group of girls?

Finally we had an idea. We suggested to Christopher what to do and settled back to watch him preserve his dignity and end the situation. Sarah came over once again and her dutiful audience giggled in anticipation of Christopher's discomfiture.

"I love you, Christopher," she crooned.

Christopher regretfully shook his head and put a protective arm around her shoulder. "I know you love me, and I don't blame you," he replied, "but Sarah, I'm looking for a *real* woman." He got up and left. Sarah sat in stunned silence. After a few moments all of us, including Sarah, were laughing.

Where Cliques Come From

How do these groups form? Most children from families of similar social standing and wealth have similar interests, so it is natural that they gravitate toward each other. In fact, peer groups often reinforce parental values because a child is likely to choose peers from his own social, educational, economic and religious background. I have always been amazed how quickly a new kid can find his appropriate peer group. They seem to have a special "radar."

Each school represented in our department has its own and more clearly defined version of the peer groups mentioned earlier. Edward Martin writes:

> One comes to school to see friends. One fears school because enemies are there also. Some of the most important parts of the school day are the walk or ride there, changing between classes, the few minutes before the class gets started, the study hall, and the end of school. These times are the intense periods of "seeing the other kids," or realizing you have no one to see.[3]

Influence of Peers—Bad and Good

Urie Bronfenbrenner has noted that the peer group

has the potential for becoming a destructive force:

> At least in the United States, the peer group tends to undermine adult socialization efforts and to encourage egocentrism, aggression, and antisocial behavior.[4]
>
> A large-scale survey of American sixth-graders found that those children who were the most peer-oriented were also those who reported engaging most often in antisocial activities such as lying to adults, smoking, and using bad language.[5]

Not only can peer groups promote undesirable behavior, but they are often responsible for repressing individual tastes, values and emotions. Many would-be musicians give up music during early adolescence because time spent practicing is not as important as time spent with friends. Girls whose one beauty is their hair will cut it, perm it, frizz it and tangle it if their friends are doing the same.

Clothes Make the Tween

Nicki was the queen bee in her clique. All the members of her group were well-dressed-designer-punk-public school girls. I remember visiting her one hot August afternoon a week before school started. She had just returned from a visit to see her father. Nicki's parents were divorced, and her dad made every effort to spoil her on her semi-annual trips. She brought out several shopping bags to show me.

"Look at this jacket," she commanded. "It was $55."

"These jeans are the latest from Italy," she said as she held them up. "Thirty-five dollars a pair and I've got three pairs."

She held up shoes, sweaters, jackets and skirts, mentioning the designer's name and the exact price of each

43

item. I felt a little sorry for her mother who was working hard just to keep the modest home for the two of them. If she had bought Nicki a pair of plain-pocket jeans, I know Nicki would have refused to wear them.

On some Sunday mornings at church I will see groups of two or three tweens wearing different versions of the same outfit. I remember one Easter when a group of friends all wore pink pumps. "You can't sit in this row," I joked with one bewildered girl who had just come into the class. "This row is reserved for pink shoes."

The Pressure to Pair Off

Although the "group" is very important, older tweenagers also have a need to be accepted by the opposite sex — and by one member of the opposite sex in particular. The tweens call it "going together," but all I ever get is a blank look when I ask them, "Where are you going?"

"Oh, Gary," is the exasperated reply. "You know what we mean."

"Going together" means that boy likes girl and girl likes boy back. They are too young to date, of course, and in our Sunday school guys and girls usually sit on opposite sides of the room. So what *do* they do? Well, the girls whisper about "her boy" and giggle a lot; the boys compliment him on his taste in women. If the young man is exceptionally brave, he may call her on the telephone once or twice. If she is unusually nervy, she may write him an occasional note.

If any tweenage parties fall during the going together period, both will be invited and they may sit together. Occasionally chaperons may find them kissing or holding hands surreptitiously. If the youth group takes a bus trip, they will undoubtedly sit together and undoubtedly bear close watching. They do what they think they are expected to do, but they have little emotional maturity and even less experience to tell them what *not* to do.

How do we view coupling at this age when statistics indicate that twelve- and thirteen-year-olds are experimenting with sex? In most instances, going together is harmless and passes quickly. During my many years of pastoring tweenagers, I have never known *any* who experimented with physical involvement beyond the level of French kissing.

"Twelve-year-olds," writes Edward Martin, "hang around in groups by sex. It is a rare exception when a member of one sex risks associating with members of the opposite sex."[6]

I have to believe, though, that a tweenager who is deeply upset and seeking either a father figure or love in any form could easily be led to experiment with sex by an older person. And of course it is not impossible for tweenagers to mimic what they see in movies and on television. But physical involvement is not a usual activity for tweenagers, particularly kids who have been reared in religious families.

Be firm with your child if he is "going" with someone. Make sure he knows about sex, its temptations and the progression which leads from affection to intercourse. Remind him that there is plenty of time for full-fledged dating, and feel free to limit opportunities for coupling.

Going together is the first taste of what is to come — a romantic relationship, his name linked with hers, a twosome, a sometimes-togetherness. It is thrilling, but at the same time it is a little unsettling and uncomfortable. Just remember that this, too, is a necessary part of growing up.

Possibility for Change

Friends mold and shape each other into mirror reflections of themselves, so peer pressure, or peer influence, can sometimes be a source for great good. Proverbs 27:17 tells us: "Iron sharpeneth iron; so a man sharpeneth the countenance of his friend." Strong Christian kids can influence their friends and encourage each other in right living.

But what can be done about the negative groups and their influence? Is there any hope for a girl or boy who wants out of an "anti-social" group?

Yes, there is. Groups change, often with astonishing rapidity. One fight over a boyfriend can send a girl scurrying from one peer group to another. Any change in a family's social status is impetus for a change of social group. If a boy or girl transfers from one school to another, he or she is certain to enter another peer group.

In fact, parents should be aware that tweenagers are the most vulnerable when they change schools. Often a kid who has never been a problem will strive to be accepted in his new school quickly. The quickest way to find peer acceptance is to attract attention—usually bad, noisy, disruptive or harmful attention. Other kids who see their wholesome lives as "boring" might decide to "change their image" and try something new. If your family is moving or if your tweenager will be changing schools, spend some extra time to ensure that your child is making a smooth transition.

Since change is possible, a wise parent or youth worker can really help a young person by seeing that they enter a group which is "on target" spiritually. You can't *dictate* this decision, but you can help in the decision-making process. If you have been teaching the principles of right and wrong rather than mandating dictatorial rules, your child will have the wisdom to discern which groups are "good" and which are "trouble." Talk to your tweenager about peer groups and how they help or hurt him. Keep your communication open and make sure your family plays an active part in your child's life.

Amy was involved with a group we call "apathetic." They sit with glum faces in Sunday school, refuse to participate in Bible memorization on Wednesday nights and generally let us know they're at church only because their parents force them to come.

Amy wanted out. She knew her friends were dragging her down spiritually, so she prayed about her situation and sought my counsel. Over the summer she was separated from her friends by a prolonged family vacation, and when the next school year began she made a conscious effort to enter a different group of girls.

Amy did well, but often I would see her struggling in Sunday school. Her old group would come in and sit behind her. As they wrote notes and quietly giggled, I could tell a part of her wanted to be with them—she wanted to talk about boys and clothes and fun, too. But Amy stuck it out and is now happy and settled with her new friends. Sure, her new friends talk about boys and clothes, but they have things in a better perspective.

How to Balance Peer Influence

Do all adolescents turn away from their parents and toward their peers at this time of life? Yes and no. Some breaking away from parental guidance and authority is natural and normal. But studies have shown that "the peer-oriented child is more a product of parental disregard than of the attractiveness of the peer group—that [the child] turns to his age mates less by choice than by default. The vacuum left by the withdrawal of parents and adults from the lives of children is filled with an undesired—and possibly undesirable—substitute of an age-segregated peer group."[7]

Quite simply, parents who take an active part in

47

their children's lives by spending time with their children will continue to have the primary influence in their tweens' lives. When the relationship between parents and children is strong, parental influence will exceed peer influence. However, parents who let their children withdraw from the family circle will allow the peer relationship to become the most important influence in a child's head and heart.

Daniel Yankelovich did a study in 1981 called "New Rules." In a recent speech, U.S. Secretary of Education William Bennett remarked on the Yankelovich study:

> He [Yankelovich] found evidence of something that should distress all of us concerned about young people. He suggests in his study that parents began to put the raising of children at a lower priority in their lives. He describes what we might call a terrible compact, a deal. As he says in his report, "We shall demand less from you, children, and in return we'll make less sacrifice for you." Yankelovich talks about the statistically demonstrable fact that many couples were less willing to stay together for the sake of their children during this period of 1960 to 1980. Yankelovich talks about an increasing tendency "for parents to say they wish to live their own lives, even if it means less time with their children."[8]

Parents must not give up their place of influence and authority in their children's lives. Members of the White House Conference on Children made the following discovery:

> The young cannot pull themselves up by their own bootstraps. It is primarily through observing, playing, and working with others older and younger than himself that a child discovers both what he can do and who he can become—that he develops both his ability and his identity. It is

primarily through exposure and interaction with adults and children of different ages that a child or adolescent acquires new interests and skills and learns the meaning of tolerance, cooperation, and compassion. Hence to relegate children to a world of their own is to deprive them of their humanity. Yet, this is what is happening in America today.[9]

What, then, is a parent to do? For starters, spend as much time as possible with your child. Begin to think of your tweenager as a very young adult and do as little as possible to embarrass him in public. In private, though, let your child know that you love him totally. Reach out for a hug even though he may pull away.

Plan some special days for your son or daughter. Make popcorn at bedtime and eat it with your daughter in her room as you talk about school and friends. Mothers, let your son take you out for lunch on a Saturday afternoon. Slip him the money before you go and allow him to order for you and pay the bill. Fathers, take your daughter out to eat at a fancy restaurant. Show her how a gentleman treats a lady.

The amount of time you spend together and the love you share does not have to change now that your child is a tween. What will change are the roles you and your child have played up to this point.

When your child was born, you placed him on a stage and glowed with happiness as an appreciative audience of friends and relatives applauded. When he walked, you stood by his side and held his hands. As he learned and grew, you were there, guiding his hands, training his mind, shaping his life. When the audience grew small and no one else applauded, you and your spouse stomped, whistled and clapped like mad for this kid you loved.

Now he is older, and your child is ready for you to

49

stand in the wings as he faces his public. Your guidance and discipline are still sorely needed in the teenage years ahead, because he is unsure of the limits of the stage. He needs your protection. But as he grows, he will find his own way and test his own limits. Your guidance and protection will no longer be needed, but take heart. Your support, love and wisdom will always be appreciated — the child, even when grown, will still need an approving audience.

4

Seeking Adulthood: "Gee, Mom, I'm too old for that!"

Gary

The young think they know everything and are confident in their assertions.

—Aristotle

You've given birth to that child, kissed his toes as you bathed him, and hugged him lovingly each time he left home for elementary school. Suddenly he withdraws from your touch, ducks his head when you reach for a kiss and forgets to call the customary "I love you!" as he leaves for school. What happened? The drive for independence has begun.

Tweenagers want to find approval from people other than their parents—namely their peers and other respected adults. The consistent love which parents have provided is suddenly "kid's stuff." In order to show themselves grown up, tweenagers feel they must turn their backs on home. It is often a painful stage for parents, but it does pass. As soon as a tweenager gains his confidence and footing in the later teenage years, he will have the maturity to acknowledge his love for home and family.

James Dobson explains the breaking-away phenomenon:

> Teenagers are engulfed by a tremendous desire to be adults, and they resent anything which implies that they are still children. When they are seen with "mommy and daddy" on a Friday night, for example, their humiliation is almost unbearable. They are not really ashamed of their parents; they are embarrassed by the adult-baby role that was more appropriate in prior years. Though it is difficult for you now, you would do well to accept this healthy aspect of growing up without becoming defensive about it. Your love relationship with your child will be reestablished in a few years, though it will never be a parent-child phenomenon again. And that's the way God designed the process to work.[1]

Tweenagers, though, don't have the hindsight necessary to understand God's process. They define independence and adulthood in their own and very unique way.

The Fear of Being a "Mama's Boy"

The greatest fear of a junior high boy is to be known as a "mama's boy" or a crybaby. Crybabies and mama's boys aren't accepted. They aren't "cool" in the social set, and they certainly aren't accepted by other boys who have established their independence and social status.

Unfortunately for those boys who are sensitive, physically small, easily embarrassed or shy about leaving the protection of home, the situation is made worse by the self-appointed bully who exists in nearly every tweenage group. What creates a bully? The desire for social acceptance and status. What makes a shy kid come back for continued harassment? The same desire for social acceptance and status.

One year Bill was in our middle school department. At twelve years of age, Bill was six feet tall and weighed about 180 pounds. He was a Christian, very sincere, and a very likable boy. But Bill was also an impossible bully. When a smaller boy entered the room, Bill somehow could never resist the urge to walk over and playfully punch the smaller boy in the stomach or slap him hard between the shoulder blades. It was Bill's way of saying, "I'm in charge here. I have power and I want you to know it."

Whenever we held physical activities or athletic games, Bill was extremely difficult to control. His desire to be the king of the mountain led him to outrageous behavior in football, basketball and swimming. He would push, shove, tackle and nearly drown the others—anything it took to establish his superiority in every field. As you can imagine, we were all relieved when Bill entered high school. I think Bill was, too. There he wasn't king of the hill, so he didn't have to constantly assert himself.

The Use of "Colorful Metaphors"

Boys not only feel this competitive drive in physical situations, but in social situations as well. They like to talk big and brag about their exploits, real or imagined. They are particularly prone to include in their language words which would cause a sailor to blush.

Recently a frantic mother came to me. "I'm a basket case," she explained. "My ten-year-old, a Christian who knows better, wrote this!"

She thrust into my hand a note the boy had written to a friend. The mother's trembling hand pointed to an unprintable profanity. How could her son have written something so vulgar?

Profanity is one of the hardest areas for a tweenage boy to control. Middle schoolers curse because they hear adults cursing on television, in the movies and, many times, at home. They curse because they want to feel and act grown up.

Kids with the best intentions try to find ways to interject a little "adult" language into their conversations. James (a strong Christian tween raised in a Christian family) and I were once talking and he used a rather questionable word. "Why, James!" I rebuked him mildly, "What kind of language is that?"

James blushed deeply. "I heard my brother say it and I tried it out on my dad and he didn't say anything."

I knew James's dad would never let something like that pass. "Your dad must not have been listening," I explained. "But I feel sure that is not a word he would like for you to be using."

Tweens curse among themselves because it is part of their own special language — a language they don't use at home or at church.

Jeremy was led to the Lord in our department, and I was pretty proud of the progress he had made. His profession of faith was real and he seemed to be trying to grow in the Lord. One day, however, I visited his public school campus and saw him standing with his group of friends. I could hear them cursing, and Jeremy was joining right in. Jeremy was too embarrassed to acknowledge to his friends that he knew me.

Some middle schoolers may curse because they don't know what is proper language and what is not.

After our country-western jamboree and its mud-fight, I was rinsing the mud from the feet of one of our middle school boys. Another boy standing nearby got too close and I accidentally splashed some water on his Reeboks. "Jee-sus Christ!" he yelled.

He gave me a look of blank innocence when I corrected him. "You mean that's wrong?" he queried.

I found it hard to believe that this kid (who had been reared in church) had never heard of "thou shalt not take the name of the Lord thy God in vain," but it was obvious he had not learned to apply the principle.

Gregory Monaco believes that the primary reason that tweens curse is their inability to express themselves:

> Take a long look at the people, especially the youths, who use foul language as a part of their vocabulary. More often than not, you will find they are unable to express their emotions (usually anger) in a constructive, honest way. Perhaps they've been told all deep emotion is wrong, or they might feel that there is too much risk to share feelings honestly. They probably have many emotions within that they don't share with anyone.
>
> Profanity, vulgarity, and foul language in general is a "safe" outlet for emotions stored inside. Verbal violence lets off steam, even commits symbolic acts of aggression, but does it from under cover. You can call someone a blankity blank and he'll never know why you're angry — just that you are. Many of the teens with whom I've worked had such low verbal skills that they substituted repetitive vulgarities for even simple concepts that they wished to communicate.[2]

Lucky for me, I suppose, I didn't get away with cursing in junior high. Once I wrote a profane note to a friend, but my mother found it. I couldn't even get away with cursing on the basketball court. My mother, who was deaf, once watched me closely during a heated exchange at a game. When I got home she lit into me: "Gary Allan Hunt," she scolded, "I saw what you said!"

Independence Through Other "Adult" Activities

Language is not the only "adult" bridge tweenagers tread upon. They also feel more "adult" when sneaking a beer or smoking cigarettes. Lawrence Kohlberg, professor of education at Harvard University, notes: "Occasionally a psychological preadolescent may take drugs, as he may drink beer or sneak cigarettes. When he does this, he does this as an activity of an exciting forbidden and grown-up variety."[3]

Kids usually start off with cigarettes. Why? Because smoking is the first assertion of "my body is my own and I will do with it as I please." Kids want to belong to the bold group whose devil-may-care attitude reflects the independence and status tweenagers admire. Smoking lends an air of toughness to boys and sophistication to girls. Look at cigarette advertising—the ads are either ultra-macho or ultra-chic. Smoking can also be a symbol of absolute rebellion. Adults warn kids about smoking and parents forbid their children to smoke, so when a child is angry and rebellious he defiantly lights up.

Angie recently interviewed U.S. Surgeon General C. Everett Koop and asked what parents could do to discourage their children from smoking. He replied:

> You can point out the fact that smoking is not a habit that you can pick up and discard when you want to. Nicotine is the most addictive drug in our society. The younger you start, the more

> difficult it is to quit. We have to point out to kids
> that there are many disadvantages — your breath
> stinks, you're not attractive to other people, and
> if you're an athlete you certainly cut down on
> your stamina. The health benefits of not smok-
> ing are tremendous.[4]

If a child never starts to smoke cigarettes, the odds are great that he will never try any drugs. Those who smoke cigarettes find it natural to move up to marijuana; of those who smoke marijuana, nearly 60 percent will go on to try other illicit drugs. If a child never smokes marijuana, the odds are ninety-eight-to-one that he or she will never try any other illegal drug.

How do you keep tweenagers from experimenting with drugs and alcohol? They have heard the horror stories about drugs and alcohol; they know they are hurting their bodies if they use such substances. But it probably wouldn't hurt to make sure young people know the following facts:

Marijuana smoke has 50 percent more tar than regular tobacco cigarettes.

Marijuana tar contains 70 percent more ben-zopyrene, a major cancer-causing chemical.

Marijuana smoke produces greater cellular changes in the lungs than does tobacco smoke.

The psychoactive chemicals in marijuana are not water soluble. They accumulate in the system and it takes about one month for all the THC (the chief intoxicant in marijuana) in one joint to leave the body. There is no other drug used or abused by man with such harmful staying power.

Marijuana isn't manly. Marijuana appears to lower normal testosterone levels in boys. (Testosterone is the major male sex hormone that is responsible for the physical changes that take place during puberty and for normal adult male sexual functioning.) In girls there are also disruptions of normal hormone levels, with possible accumulation of marijuana's chemicals in the ovaries.[5]

Alcohol can make a kid throw up, miss the best part of the party and ruin his new car. Alcohol causes teenagers to vegetate, regurgitate and urinate. It can give a hangover, put a brain to sleep and create a drug addict (some teenagers become alcoholics within six months after taking their first drink.) Alcohol can destroy a kid's liver, get him in trouble with the law and hurt his heart. Alcohol can interfere with teens' reproductive systems, wreck their cars and kill their friends—more than 12,000 young Americans are killed each year in auto accidents involving alcohol. Forty thousand more are disfigured. Alcohol can make anyone act like an idiot. It can tear a family apart. It can kill. Sure, alcohol can make a teenager feel like everyone else at a party, but who wants to be like a group that is mindless, bombed, wasted and dumb?[6]

It's sad, but when tweens see their *parents* smoke, drink and overeat, they reason that a little bit won't hurt them. They feel good inside when they use drugs and feeling good is precious when feeling insecure is the alternative.

Before I became a Christian I was a heavy drug user. I have my personal experience to share with kids and I can relate to where they are coming from. My kids know that I understand what drugs are like and how they can ruin a life. But, most important, they know that I really care about them. Because I really love them, they don't question my motives for standing against drugs.

It is almost impossible to "preach" a kid out of drug use. It is very difficult for parents to "plead" a kid out of drug use. The best way for parents or youth workers to keep tweenagers away from any drug is to make sure that their tweens are secure enough so they don't need drugs to feel good or grown up.

Adulthood Equals Privileges

Tweenagers drink and smoke and swear because these are "adult" privileges which they can assume without too much difficulty. Unlike adults, who measure maturity by how one handles responsibility, *tweenagers measure maturity by privileges, granted or taken.* The tremendous drive for independence which begins during the tweenage years is really the desire for the status of adulthood, with all the "privileges" tweenagers covet: the freedom to drive (controlling one's physical surroundings), the freedom from school (controlling one's mental surroundings), the freedom to choose their own friends and circumstances (controlling one's social surroundings.)

When your tweenagers are tempted to seek adulthood through unwise behaviors, stress that maturity is not a matter of being able to do what you please, but doing what pleases God, even when the odds are against you. But don't simply pronounce a list of "thou shalt not's." Instead, teach your children the *principles* behind your rules. Teach that true freedom is the ability to choose to do right, not the freedom to do wrong.

Freedom does not automatically arrive at age eighteen or twenty-one when young people can vote, gamble, and buy cigarettes and beer. True freedom and maturity arrives when a young person develops character that will withstand the tests of the world.

Through the media and his peers your tweenager is told that grown-up glamour is within his reach. Parents and youth workers must stress that real maturity is also within his reach — it consists of following God's plans and principles.

5

The Emotional Roller Coaster

Angie

Am I the person who used to wake in the middle of the night and laugh with the joy of living? Who worried about the existence of God and danced with the young ladies till the lark-light? Who sang Auld Lang Syne and howled with sentiment, and more than once gazed at the full moon through a blur of great, romantic tears?

—Logan Pearsall Smith

We were at camp. The speaker had just finished a stirring and convicting message, and I was counseling a girl who came down the aisle in tears. "I want to do better," she sobbed. "I know the Lord wants me to spend more time in prayer and Bible study, but it's so hard! I'm going to promise the Lord never to miss a daily quiet time again."

I prayed with her and secretly hoped that she would

honor her commitment. I had seen too many tweenagers make sudden fervent promises at an emotional moment and fall by the wayside only a few weeks later.

Each Sunday morning and Wednesday night I would ask her how she was doing. "Fine," she would answer, quickly trying to avoid any further questions. A few months later she decided to level with me.

"I've stopped reading my Bible. I feel like my prayers don't go any higher than the ceiling. I wonder if God is there at all. I know I was saved, I remember it clearly, but there are days when God just isn't real to me."

The tweenage years are a sudden merging of childish and adult emotions. Like a cup of cold water thrown on a hot skillet, these emotions burn and sizzle with fierce intensity then die away. Love, hate, devotion, anger, jealousy and happiness burn one minute and vanish the next.

What causes the emotional upheaval of the tweenage years? The child prior to adolescence experienced emotions as a result of *external* activities or objects: a child was unhappy because certain events were bad; he felt love because people gave to him; he felt excitement because an activity was fun. At the onset of adolescence, however, the child begins to experience emotions which have their root in his *internal* being.

These new emotions are bewildering. Girls cannot understand why they feel moody and depressed at the time of their monthly period, and mothers and fathers who question "What's wrong?" don't help. The girls themselves do not know what is wrong.

Last Sunday Gary and I crept into church late and sat in a packed pew next to one of our middle school girls. Gary leaned over, caught her eye and murmured a greeting.

She lowered her head and began to sob—racking,

shaking sobs—with no sound, only tears. I turned to him, bewildered, and asked, "What on earth did you say to her?"

"I said 'hi'," he answered. "Maybe I scared her."

As we sat in the crowded pew I could feel her small body sobbing through the special music, the announcements and the offertory hymn. During prayer time I scrawled on an envelope and passed it to her: "Honey, is there something wrong? Is there anything I can pray about with you?"

She looked up and shook her head. I looked down the pew—her mother and sister were sitting on the other side and they did nothing but cast clinical glances. They knew what was wrong; apparently our little middle school girl was simply upset from some family fight.

Life has its vicissitudes, but they are magnified during the tweenage years. Joy, pain, sorrow, happiness—tweenagers delight in exploring these new emotions. They will listen to the latest hit record over and over again because the song will either lift them to new heights of joy or plunge them into delicious depths of melancholy. Drugs are often used to experience new highs and lows. Girls devour romance novels to enjoy exciting, vicarious love affairs.

These new emotions are powerful and difficult to control. Anger, rebellion and fear can explode into physical fighting. Fits of anger often result in teary explosions during which time it is impossible to reason with the tweenager. Let the anger subside, then try to sound out the web of emotions and circumstances which caused the outburst. Tweenagers may not know exactly why they feel a certain way, but they want someone wiser and older to understand that they *don't* understand.

Life at the Mercy of Emotions

A tweenager's commitment, whether to home,

63

Christ or an athletic team, may be at the mercy of these ever-changing emotions. Those who work with tweenagers must be sure that commitments are based upon *fact,* not feeling. Facts do not change; feelings evaporate rapidly and often without reason.

Several years ago Gary worked with a young man we'll call Chip. Chip's father lived in another state and Chip's relationship with his stepfather was not good. Gary discipled Chip on a regular basis and Chip's growth as a new Christian thrilled us. One night we watched proudly as eighth-grade Chip walked the aisle and informed the church that he felt called of God to the youth ministry.

Chip then left our department and our contact with him was limited. Gary would occasionally drop him a note or stop by to see him, but Chip's mother was going through another divorce and the household was in turmoil. Chip moved away from home into an apartment with an unsaved young man.

The other night we saw Chip again. His hair was shaved except for a strip down the back of his head — that remaining hair was orange, red and black. He wore a couple of earrings and black leather. He smiled and said hello; we did the same.

When we got home, Gary wrote Chip a letter and gently reminded him of the commitment he made while in the eighth grade. Gary ended with, "If you need anything, please don't hesitate to call" and prayed that Chip would take the time to contact him sometime.

What happened to Chip? What will happen to Chip in the future? We don't know. We only know that his case illustrates a valid point — if a tweenager is given time, love and attention, he can be led in the right way. When he is denied those crucial elements, commitments can be forgotten or forsaken. Responsibilities are also at the mercy of emotions. Surely you can recall a time in your childhood when you were supposed to clean your room, but a friend came by with a new record and somehow your chore never got done. Or perhaps you were supposed to pick up your brother from school, but you were so upset at failing your math test you walked home in deep gloom, completely forgetting your sibling.

I'm not saying that tweenagers shouldn't have responsibilities – they should. But parents, don't expect your child to have the mental acuity to keep her affairs perfectly in order. She will make mistakes. When she does, have her rectify her mistake and begin again.

Tweenage Worrywarts

Probably the most consistent emotional state in the tweenage years is worry. Tweenagers worry a lot.

Claudia, a sixth-grader, says she worries about "not getting a date." She won't be allowed to date for several years, but she's worrying about it now!

Mike, an eighth-grader, says he worries about "getting rejected by friends and getting laughed at."

Tweens worry about friends, money, family and growing up; they worry about getting decent grades, getting pimples, being fat, being clumsy and being left out. They worry that they will never have a boyfriend or girlfriend, that their freckles are too prevalent, or that their clothes are too old or too outdated. They worry about going to hell, never being able to drive a car and being embarrassed in public.

Boys worry about not making the team. Being part of the team is a status symbol – it means you have worth, that you are good, desirable and a cut above the ordinary. If a boy makes the team he worries about making a mistake, costing the team the game or looking funny as he plays the sport. He feels clumsy, disjointed and awkward.

He worries that if he gets hurt he will cry—the embarrassment of crying is worse than the pain of injury. He worries that he will be called "sissy" by the coach or the other players. He worries that his father won't be proud of him or care enough to come to the game.

The boys in our department often play a game we call "murderball." The objective is simple: Get your opponent out by hitting him with a large, soft-rubber ball. Half the boys are on one side of the gym, the other half are on the other side of the center court line, and three kickballs are given to each team. The balls are thrown at the opposing team. If the ball hits a man, he is out and must retire to the sidelines. If the ball is caught by an opposing man before it bounces, the boy who threw the ball must leave the game.

I was reading an essay by Thomas Cottle and found that he often played murderball (he called the game "bombardment") as an adolescent in the late 1940s. He recalls the worries of an adolescent boy:

> I feared for my face, for my hands and genitals and gut. It was my back and buttocks, I prayed, that would take the punishment. I could not, however, face up to this torture, I mean literally advance head on into this salvo of cruelty and aggression. But I never told a single human being of my fright. Not one single person knew my terror. I simply didn't want to get hurt, but I did feel strongly that if I could just bonk a few guys with that hard rubber ball, maybe even sink one of their lungs when they caught my throw, I'd be in good shape. I would be a better man for it. I would, perhaps, be a man.[1]

Cottle also remembered what it was like to play basketball, "shirts" against "skins":

Why was it so embarrassing, this exposure of skin and the display of our chests and backs? Some of us had acne and that was humiliating, but I think more than anything it was that physically we simply were not up to the ideal stature and the ideal posture, size, and strength. The ideal was evidently present in all of our minds.[2]

Girls worry about looking "right." They worry about their clothes and their friends. Girls are jealous when a new girl comes to school: What if the new girl takes away her best friend? What happens if her boyfriend decides to like the new girl? If mother buys daughter a new dress and daughter doesn't know of someone—an "acceptable" someone—who has one just like it or nearly like it, she is hesitant to wear it no matter how pretty or well-made it is.

Girls worry about sports—they hate to be the last one chosen when team captains are choosing teams. They gaze wistfully at the more developed older girls and wish their breasts would hurry and grow. Girls worry about the spurt of growth which causes them to grow taller than the boys their age and stretches their feet longer than they are supposed to be. Girls worry about starting their periods in school or in front of a boy; they worry about wearing a bra or not wearing one because they must undress in front of others for gym class.

Worries at School

Elizabeth says, "I worry about my grades. I get upset when I see a *C* or a *D*. I think, *I could have studied more,* or *What a foolish, careless mistake.*"

Since many schools begin tracking, or phasing, in middle school, another area for concern is developed. Students who find themselves in the group of "intelligent" students worry that they will not be able to maintain elevated status. Students who have been relegated to the lower

67

tracks resent the inference that they are sub-normal. They often rationalize their low placement: "School isn't important anyway." A student who develops this attitude is likely to carry it with him throughout his educational career.

Worries at Church

Church can also provide occasions for worry. Our middle school department has an organized singing group called "The Light Company." They often travel on weekends and sing in other churches. Occasionally we schedule them to provide the music in our own Sunday school department.

On any other Sunday our kids come into the classroom early so they can meet and talk with their friends. But on Sundays when The Light Company is scheduled to sing, one-fourth of the group purposely arrives late so they won't have to sing in front of their peers. Another fourth will conveniently "forget" to wear their group outfits. Singing in front of strange adults is easy, but singing in front of friends is so embarrassing that our tweens try to avoid it at all costs.

Worries at Home

Church and school provide many opportunities for a tweenager to worry. Unfortunately, a lot of tweenagers worry about their homes as well:

"When my parents fight, I worry that they'll be getting a divorce and I'll have to choose between them."

"My older sister keeps threatening to kill herself. I feel like I should do something, but I don't know what to do."

"My kid brother gets all the attention. I really don't care anymore, but I used to worry that my parents didn't love me as much as they loved him."

"My parents are always saying 'we can't afford it.'

Sometimes I worry we won't be able to pay the bills or that we'll have to move out of our house."

"My dad is always sick, or at least he says he is. I'm worried that he's going to die."

"My mother drinks constantly. I think she's an alcoholic, and I worry that she'll hurt herself someday. She might even hurt somebody else."

"I think my brother is using drugs. His friends don't seem all that great to me, but he likes them better than he likes us. I'm afraid he's going to end up in jail."

Home — the place which should bring welcome relief from the cares of a harsh and demanding world — is often the source of greatest pressure and worry for a tweenager. How about your home? Obviously no family exists without some pressures and difficulties, but when those difficulties come do you resort to worry or to prayerful faith? What is the example you are setting for your children?

Like a gentle flower which exists for only a twelve-hour period, this time of budding emotion in your tweenager should be cherished. It is a time of newness, awakening and increasing awareness. Expose your child to the beauty of human emotion. When difficulties come, lead him by your example.

6

Rebel With a Cause

Angie

Youth on the prow, and pleasure at the helm.
— Thomas Gray

Dare we suggest it? There is a cloud behind the silver lining of parenthood: rebellion. Full-scale rebellion, not unlike the temper tantrums of a two-year-old, rears its ugly head in the tweenage years.

Although a certain degree of rebellion is natural and to be expected, many parents are caught off guard by the constant battle of wills with their tweenagers. The child who has always been trustworthy may suddenly begin to lie to his parents so that he can go along with the peer group he now reveres as his ultimate authority.

In *Parents and Teenagers,* Dr. Grace Ketterman writes:

> The biggest challenge a teenager has is to develop his own personal identity and establish

his independence. If not given a chance to break free from the dominance of his parents, at least to a degree, he is likely to face problems as he becomes interdependent with others during dating, marriage, and parenting. Unless teenagers are given a chance to explore and establish their own beliefs, values, and behavior while they still have parents to guide them, they tend to turn to their peers for that guidance. I would rather see a teen rebel a little against parents than become overly subservient to the wrong kind of peers.[1]

Why do tweenagers rebel? Aside from the rather inconsequential rebellion which results primarily from "testing" parental standards, rebellion on a more severe scale results from a "broken promise." A study by Arthur L. Stinchcombe[2] showed that adolescents believe certain behaviors should earn certain results. For instance, good performance in school should result in good grades; good grades should result in parental approval. When the expected chain of events is broken and the unspoken promise is not kept, the adolescent rebels against the "system" and refuses to try again. *If the system doesn't work,* he reasons, *why should I try? Why should I try my best — which is supposed to get me good grades, which are supposed to guarantee a good college, which is supposed to guarantee a secure job, which is supposed to guarantee a successful future — if the system doesn't work? I tried my best and I didn't get good grades!*

The broken promise can be in any area — family, school, spiritual life. Many times we've had to deal with rebellious tweenagers whose parents have just gone through a divorce: "I tried to be good and make it easier for Mom and Dad, but they split anyway." Other tweenagers may be angry at God for the death of a parent: "God promised to take care of us and He took away my mom."

An adolescent who experiences this total rebellion against the system sees no use in preparing for any sort of future. All that he has been brought up to believe has failed. He can see no use in self-restraint or good performance. All that matters, he reasons, is finding pleasure and happiness for the moment. There is no trustworthy promise for the future.

Dealing With Rebellion

How do you handle rebellion? It is important to realize that severe rebellion is not a sudden action but a gradual process. As your child advances through the years of early adolescence, he learns that he is truly "in between": He is expected to be much more than a child but much less than an adult. He encounters frustrations when he attempts either grown-up or childish behaviors. How he handles those frustrations will determine whether he accepts his position in life or rebels against it.

Communication Is the Key

As you see your child begin to grow toward maturity and independence, make it a priority to keep communication open. Take your son or daughter out to McDonald's for a Coke and a hamburger, and encourage him or her to talk! Shopping won't do it and neither will a movie. Consciously make opportunities to simply have a good talk with your tween.

Find out what bothers your tweenager and discern his reactions to his problems. Discuss how to handle anger, hurt and disappointment. Show him by your example that maturity involves knowing how to handle life's "bumps" without bitterness. Share with him the peace, joy, faith and self-control of the Holy Spirit. If necessary, be ready to explain why a "broken promise" is no reason for quitting in life. Use your wisdom and maturity to help the child learn that the promise was broken due to circumstances beyond his control.

Most of us would never dream of ignoring our mate if he or she came home angry or hurt, but so many parents ignore their children when they are upset! Somehow we get the idea that young people only have small, inconsequential problems, so we don't probe behind the closed door or wonder why Johnny has no appetite at dinner. We think that kids' problems are rather easily solved or forgotten. We find it easier to take the child shopping to "take his mind off it" than to sit down and make a concentrated effort to talk about the problem.

When you talk with your tweenager about his rebellion, be sure to convey the following messages:

1. You've noticed changes in him that have perplexed you. If you have responded incorrectly or ignored the problem, apologize.

2. Adolescence is a period of change, and frustration is built in to the tweenage years! Although he is facing pressures unlike the ones you faced, you love him tremendously and will do all you can to help him through these years.

3. He is growing toward maturity and soon he will be on his own with total freedom, responsible only to God. As he grows, his freedom at home will increase more and more, but on a timetable established by you, his parents.

4. He is not grown yet! As much as he'd like to be able to do entirely as he pleases, he cannot have the freedom of an adult while still a tweenager. What he wants is the best of two worlds—the irresponsibility of childhood and the freedom of adulthood.

5. You are responsible to God for his safety, well-

being and spiritual development. Let your child know that you will try to be more receptive to his feelings and needs, and that you will carefully consider any new requests for privileges. But there will be times when you, as a parent, must say no. When that happens, your child should know that no amount of whining or pouting will change that decision. As parents, you will strive to be fair and firm.[3]

Approach Your Tween Now

Those of us who have worked with tweenagers have seen kids who, even at this early age, have tremendous chips on their shoulders which alienate them from our efforts to reach them. Eddie is one such young man. He's bright, physically advanced for his age and a leader in his peer group. But any efforts of ours to engage him in friendly conversation or simple fun are quietly rebuffed. He argues simply for the sake of arguing. His countenance is never open or joyous—it is always sullen and distant.

Gary has talked to Eddie's father, who is unaware that Eddie has a problem. Either Eddie is adept at hiding his feelings at home, or his parents simply assume that his moodiness is a passing phase.

I've seen enough young men and women like Eddie to know that unless someone probes deep enough to find out what the broken promise or disappointment is, Eddie will only grow more and more detached and spiritually cold. It is possible that someday Eddie will hear a sermon or learn a spiritual truth that will help him analyze his own problem, but it is a shame that so many years will be wasted in indifference and silent rebellion.

If you see that your child has been hurt or disappointed, sit him down for a heart-to-heart talk *immediately*. Don't allow the problem to fester thinking "Oh, he'll get over it in time." Unresolved hurt encourages the development of indifference.

If the mask of indifference is already imprinted onto your child's face and your efforts to talk to him have failed, I strongly suggest that you find a Christian counselor who will be able to win his confidence and find the root problem. Your pastor, a respected teacher or youth pastor may be able to help. Just make sure your child respects the counselor and that the counselor is going to treat your child with the same respect.

Most importantly, if your tween's rebellion is more than you can handle, be willing to admit that your child has a problem. There is more to rebellion than breaking rules, flaunting authority, and screaming arguments. These loud and disruptive behaviors are only symptoms of other underlying problems. Tweenagers generally will not rebel against people they respect, so keep your tween's respect by taking the time to show you care.

Explain the Principles Behind Your Rules

For the rebellion which is really a "testing" of parental authority, talk about your rules, guidelines and standards, and explain *why* you hold these standards. Don't patronize or antagonize your child — remember that he is learning to think for himself. Your reasons for disallowing an activity must be founded on biblical principles. Rules without underlying principles are sure to be broken.

For example: Mr. and Mrs. Jones do not want their daughter to date non-Christian boys. But instead of offering a reason when their daughter questions, "Why not?", they simply respond, "Because we said so. That's reason enough."

Their daughter will adhere to the rule as long as she thinks she may get caught. However, if the occasion arises or if she is away from home, she may happily take up with a young man of whom she knows her parents would not approve. Aside from the objection of her parents, which she has disallowed, she does not see a valid reason why she shouldn't.

Mr. and Mrs. Jones need to explain their principles behind the rule: "We would prefer that you not date non-Christians because every date is a potential mate. We also feel that in order to have a mature and fulfilling relationship you must be able to relate to your boyfriends not only on a mental and social level, but also on a spiritual level." Their daughter would now understand their rule and be more willing to consider their standard as a permanent principle for her life.

I taught twelfth-grade English in a Christian school one year and was surprised to hear that three of my former students had run amuck after graduation. As soon as they were free from the rules of the school (and since they were eighteen, they felt they were free from their parents' rules, too), they spent their nights in bars and nightclubs, wildly seeking what they thought they had been denied. What the rebels were actually lacking was a set of principles they could believe in through all of life's situations. They had heard such principles, I am sure—they simply had never integrated the principles into their own lives. When the rules ended, so did their convictions.

As you talk with your tweenagers, don't just describe rules and the penalties for breaking them. Discuss the principles which support the guidelines. Make sure your tweenager understands your consistent support and the inevitability of your discipline if the guidelines are not followed.

When it comes time to discipline your tween, maintain honest communication and safeguard his trust. Make sure the circle of confession is only as large as the circle of transgression. Don't make the broken rule and subsequent punishment a matter of public record.

Keeping Rebellion to a Minimum

How can a parent bring up a child so that problems with rebellion will be minimal? By teaching through example and attitude the principles of authority.

Each of us has a higher authority. As citizens we are under the authority of the laws of this country; as Christians we are all under the authority of God and His Word.

Parents and youth leaders who show a healthy respect for authority and the rights of others will impart that respect to their children. Parents who attend worship regularly and financially support their church will teach their children to respect God. Most important, parents who respect and apologize to their children and to each other when necessary will illustrate that only God is infallible. We owe our ultimate obedience to Him.

My husband always teases me because I was engaged two times during my teenage years. I couldn't help it — I was (like most girls) young, romantic and totally in love with each of the special young men I was engaged to. Though I only had stars in my eyes, my parents, fortunately, had wisdom in their hearts.

After praying and seeking God's will for my life, my folks flatly forbade me on both occasions to marry the young man to whom I had promised my heart at the time. Though you may be sure I cried, pleaded and rationalized my reasons behind my commitment, in the end I knew I had to abide by the wishes of my parents. I had been brought up with the simple verse, "Children, obey your parents." I felt God would not honor a marriage made against the wishes of my mom and dad.

Waiting for God's best wasn't always easy, but I found it when I met my husband at college. I was twenty-two; he was twenty-nine. Given our age difference, we would never have met in high school, but in His timing God worked His plan in our lives.

So parents, raise your children in the protection of the principle of obedience. The emotional, independent and often rebellious thinking of tweenagers needs that firm foothold. Their obedience and your wise guidance will see them through.

7

Physical Changes

Gary

---

*My eleven-year-old daughter mopes around the
house all day waiting for her breasts to grow.*
— *Bill Cosby*

If you're not beguiling by age twelve, forget it.
— *Lucy Van Pelt from Peanuts (Charles Schulz)*

I was a late bloomer. I didn't shave until I was nearly twenty, never grew hair on my chest until I was a legal
adult, and spoke falsetto voice until I was well into my
teenage years. I was a short, sensitive, redheaded kid who
cried easily and was picked on constantly. One day I decided
that I would toughen up and I actively fought back. Coin-
cidentally or not, I began to grow and "Squeaky Hunt" became one of the loudest and most aggressive fighters on the
block.

In a typical middle school department you will encounter the complete spectrum of adolescent physical development. Many girls will be rail-thin wispy stalks of childhood; other girls the same age will carry themselves with the assurance of womanly dignity. Among twelve-year-old boys you will find boys with five o'clock shadow and others who are four feet tall with pre-peach fuzz. The range of development is large and those in advanced puberty are as likely to be embarrassed about their growth as those at the slow end of development.

Furthermore, teenagers today are physically maturing faster than we did. James Dobson notes this development:

> Statistical records indicate that our children are growing taller today than in the past, probably resulting from better nutrition, medicine, exercise, rest, and recreation. And this more ideal physical environment has apparently caused sexual maturity to occur at younger and younger ages. It is thought that puberty in a particular child is "turned on" when he reaches a certain level of growth; therefore, when environmental circumstances propel him upward at a faster rate, he becomes sexually mature much earlier. For example, in 1850, the average age of menarche (first menstruation) in Norwegian girls was 17.0 years of age; in 1950 it was 13.0. The average age of puberty had dropped four years in that one century. In the United States, the average age of menarche dropped from 14.2 in 1900 to 12.9 in 1950. More recent figures indicate the average has now dropped closer to 12.6 years of age! Thus, the trend toward younger dating and sexual awareness is a result, at least in part, of this physiological mechanism.[1]

As you observe tweenagers, you will notice that girls mature physically at a faster rate than boys. Girls usually begin their menstrual cycles between ages ten and twelve;

boys are usually thirteen or fourteen before they begin to show signs of change. Dr. Grace Ketterman discusses boys' development:

> The changes in boys are slower, later, and less extreme. They begin to get a little hair on their faces, but it doesn't become heavy for several years. Their voices lower, which is probably the most noticeable change and often embarrasses them. But the most alarming development that boys encounter is the nocturnal emission. This sign is an evidence that they are beginning to develop the ability to become fathers some day, but many parents don't think to explain to their sons what is taking place.[2]

Sex Education: Why and When

It is important that parents and youth leaders explain the tremendous physical changes that are about to take place. *Someone* must do it. Parents who are shy about frankly talking about sex may ask a youth leader to talk privately to their child. Tweenagers will learn about sex sooner or later, and it is better for a young person to learn about sex from someone who can explain God's plan. Sex, and talking about sex, is like a piece of sod—beautiful only in its proper place.

Some time ago a girl I had pastored in junior high sat crying in my office. She was eighteen and pregnant. Her parents had no idea they had a grandchild on the way. They would never be able to believe that their darling Christian daughter had engaged in premarital sex. They had never given her sexuality a serious thought or more than perfunctory attention at home. She had received the standard lecture when she was twelve, and even though sexual pressure in her life continued throughout her dating years, her parents assumed she knew enough and was strong enough to withstand any temptation.

In the climate of today's sexually promiscuous society, sex education has to begin in the cradle. Clifford and Joyce Penner, authors of *A Gift for All Ages,* suggest beginning sex education when children are learning the names of the parts of their bodies. "Call a penis a penis and a vagina a vagina," say the Penners, "even if it shocks the grandparents. Giving children correct anatomical names for genitals will help them develop the attitude that genitals are as valid and acceptable a part of their bodies as their toes, fingers, and nose."[3]

Surgeon General Koop recently gave Angie advice about when to teach sex education:

> As soon as youngsters begin to talk and ask questions, they have a concern and interest in their own anatomy and where babies come from. When they get to be about six, they lose interest in sex until they are about nine. You don't have to worry much about them between six and nine. But when they are nine, they really begin to develop a curiosity and this is the ideal time to teach children.
>
> Teach them before they themselves become involved in adolescence and are very concerned about their own sexuality. At that point you're not teaching the abstract, but something that they are deeply involved with and very embarrassed to talk about.[4]

A good sex education program begins before your child starts to mature physically. But no matter what you have done in the past, complete your child's education now!

Your explanations don't have to give a complete and graphic description of every sexual act and term. Your child needs to know how pregnancy occurs. He or she also needs to know the difference between kissing and petting. The most common complaint I hear from older teens is "My parents told me that going all the way was too far, but they never said anything about what I could do along the way!" Explain to your children that men are sexually stimulated by sight, women by touch. Young girls can understand the principles behind modest clothing when they understand that most males find skimpy clothing an actual physical turn-on.

Parents, be aware that your sexual attitudes are transmitted to your children. If a nine-year-old who is suddenly sexually curious has noticed that his parents seem to be hesitant about kissing in front of him or embarrassed about sexual matters, he will not bring his questions to them.

Recently Angie counseled a young college woman who hates men. "My mother hates sex anyway," she said. "One day she sat me down and told me all about sex and then said, 'Whew. I'm glad that's over.' Later I asked her if she enjoyed sex and she grimaced and said, 'I really could do without it.'"

Questions about sex should be answered truthfully and to the extent that the young person wants to know. "The Talk" should not be a one-time event, but several smaller discussions about physical maturation, physical attraction, dating behavior, etc. Above all, sex should be presented as a natural and God-given gift intended for marriage.

Sex education has to be taught with accompanying moral guidelines.*   If sex education is offered without

---

*One of the best books we have seen for junior high and high school boys and girls is *Sex: Desiring the Best* (Here's Life Publishers, 1987) by popular youth speakers Barry St. Clair and Bill Jones. This book along with its companion volumes titled *Dating: Picking (and Being) a Winner* and *Love: Making It Last* present a healthy, respectful view of biblical sexuality in the language of today's young person.

values, the education becomes lessons in sexual techniques. It is like teaching an eleven-year-old how to drive a car: You present the car, explain its parts, tell him there is no experience quite like it, and then hope that he waits until he is sixteen to drive. If he's not given solid reasons to wait, he won't.

There's No "Shield" From Society

Realistically, I know that every parent will not tell his child what he needs to know about sex. As a youth pastor, I have found that I tread a precarious line between intervening and interfering. "Let the church teach the kids about living godly lives," many parents challenge. But if a child comes to me with questions about *sex* and I give him answers, I may have an angry phone call later that night: "Some matters belong in the privacy of our home. How dare you teach my son about sex — I'm trying to shield him from it!"

Any parent who believes that children can be "shielded" from sex is not awake in the twentieth century. Practically every sitcom on television explores a sexual theme periodically, if not weekly. At best, they offer the message "Sex is fine when you're *older* and prepared to be *responsible.*"

Condom advertising is now on television and carried in *Sporting News* and on billboards. Norm Geisler, one of the great intellectuals of our generation and a professor at Dallas Theological Seminary, recently talked with Angie about the movement to advertise birth control devices and encourage young people to have "responsible sex":

> We have 1.1 million teenage pregnancies each year and 39 percent of those girls kill their babies. Sixty percent of the remaining ones go on welfare. If we encourage more people to use birth

control, the ten percent failure rate which exists across the board will automatically be doubled. You will double the number of illegitimate births, and the number of abortions, and will simply add to the problem instead of solving it.[5]

AIDS has become a household word and is quite certainly a national threat. Think a moment. If you knew one pregnant, unmarried teenager in the last five years, in the next ten years you will probably know a teenager with AIDS. AIDS is spreading rapidly among those who practice uninformed, "unsafe" sex — and teenagers are at high risk.

No, we cannot afford to shield our children from sex education. We also cannot afford to simply let them absorb the sexual messages which surround them.

What Society is Saying

Today's tweenagers are growing up in a world where many responsible and admired adults scoff at chastity or consider abstinence too much to ask of young people. The word "virgin" is hurled as an insult. Sex sells everything from toothpaste to blue jeans. As Christian parents and youth leaders, we cannot afford to ignore or whitewash the sexual temptations which profoundly affect our tweenagers.

Judy Blume is an author with an avid following among early adolescents. Even kids who hate to read will read her books because she speaks their language and deals with topics kids always want to know about but don't always want to ask about: menstruation, masturbation, premarital sex, etc. In a recent article in *Family Circle*, Blume shared letters she received from tweenagers about sex:

Dear Judy:
    I'm in eighth grade. Do you think thirteen is

87

too young to date? My parents think it is. All my friends have been going out since seventh grade at least . . . I'd do anything to be popular.

Shona, age thirteen

Dear Judy:

How does a girl kiss a boy—arms around the neck or waist? Also, do you squeeze the lips real hard, and are the girl's lips placed exactly on the boy's or is the girl's upper lip above the boy's upper lip, or what?

Melanie, age eleven

Dear Judy:

Boys are a problem and so is virginity. I like boys but will not go far. Most people at school think you are weird if you are in the eighth grade and a virgin. I think it is something I want to save for marriage.

All my feelings build up inside of me because I can't talk about them with my mom and I'm too shy to do so with my friends. I think I am over-weight, but do not know. I'm very lonely.

Stacey, age fourteen

But the advice Blume gives to tweens is typical of our societal mindset:

Both boys and girls should be responsible for preventing unwanted pregnancies. If you do decide to have intercourse, use birth control. Go to a doctor or a family-planning clinic before you do it . . . If you're worried about spontaneity, about romance, about just letting whatever happens, happen—then you're not mature enough to handle intercourse. It's up to you to take control. It's your body. It's your life.[6]

But the bodies of Christians are not our own, for we

are bought with a price. We are not in control of our lives for we serve Another. These are the teachings which are missing in the secular presentation of "responsible sex."

Sexuality in the Life of a Tween

A tweenager's social, emotional, spiritual and mental state is profoundly affected by his or her body. Girls face the greatest sexual temptation in the tweenage years because they mature faster and are attracted to older teenage boys. Girls are told that upon menstruation they will become women. It's a heady feeling to wake up one morning a "woman" when you were a girl playing with dolls the day before. A girl's body tells her she is mature. Her mother suddenly instigates secret and serious woman-to-woman talks. And her father hesitates to draw her onto his lap. In her heart, though, a girl misses those afternoons of quiet and silly girlhood when the world was uncomplicated. Now she is expected to know how to kiss, to make a boy like her and to keep a boy interested at all costs.

Sexual matters are not the first concern of tweenage boys, however. "The boy's world," writes J. M. Tanner of the University of London, "is one where *physical* powers bring prestige as well as success, where the body is very much an instrument of the person."[7] Tweenage boys find that physical prowess either ensures them a high position on the social ladder or condemns them to "shrimp" status. Sexual maturity is not crucial at this age; athletic ability is what counts. The tweenage years can be difficult indeed for boys whose biological clocks are behind their peers'.

When those growth hormones start to flow, though, watch out! Paul D. Meier, author of *Christian Child-Rearing and Personality Development,* describes his fourteenth year:

I grew ten inches in about fifteen or sixteen

89

months. I was so awkward for a while that relatives quit inviting our family over for dinner — among other things I broke glasses, a camera, and my uncle's pool cue, mostly because I misjudged how long my arms and legs were. And I bumped my head so many times on low overheads that I'm surprised I don't have any residual brain damage![8]

He was lucky. I was so uncoordinated that I fell twice — on two separate occasions — into the deep end of an empty pool. I still have little dents in my head where pebbles were imbedded.

Whenever you wonder if you are going to make it through this tweenage parenting experience, remember what you put your parents through!

Your tweenager may be frightened of these upcoming physical changes. If you don't explain the physical developments before they appear, your child could be scared out of his wits when they arrive. Even if you do explain them thoroughly and completely, your child may still worry about *when* the events will happen, so keep the lines of communication open.

Avoid teasing your tweenager. Let him or her know that physical developments will come in time. Each person is on an individual timetable — that's the way God created us. Physical maturation is a wonderful part of His plan.

8

Mental Mayhem

Gary

A boy's will is the wind's will, And the thoughts of youth are long, long thoughts.
— Longfellow

As reason is a Rebel unto Faith,
so Passion unto Reason.
— Sir Thomas Browne

I was in the seventh grade and suffering through geometry. Whenever the teacher launched into a lengthy explanation, I launched into my favorite daydream:

"There are only two seconds to go in this game and the opposition has the ball. It's a pass—no, wait! Hunt, the rising young star from Ohio, has intercepted the ball! He's dribbling down the court—what a flash of lightning! He's defending himself expertly and the opposition has double-teamed the man! It's an incredible job he's doing, but he's too far down the court to try for a shot. The clock is running out—what? No! Yes! Hunt has just shot what has to be the world's longest goal and it was a perfect swoosh! The Ohio team wins! The applause is deafening. His teammates are carrying young Hunt off the court and into the locker room where the press is waiting. What a star!"

Fantasy Island

Practically every tweenage boy and girl have entertained some version of the above daydream. To be a star—that is the unspoken desire of every adolescent. Within each heart is the precious hope that he or she will be the one in a million who rises to fame and fortune as a rock star, a movie star, an athletic wonder or a brilliant television personality.

The children who used to play with dolls and toy trucks have simply moved their fantasies from toys to daydreams. In this silent, secret world and in the privacy of their bedrooms, tweenagers sing into hairbrushes in front of the mirror, shoot paper wads into imaginary basketball hoops, and leap over chairs and trash cans carrying an invisible football over an imaginary goal line. Girls toss their hair teasingly over the shoulders and dreamily kiss the mirror thinking of the day when it will be real. Boys primp and flex in their underwear.

Imagination is fueled by the exciting prospects of reality—"I *am* growing up! I *can* be a star! I can be whatever I want to be!" Of course the tweenager's emotions often hamper his mental processes and his imagination, but he is moving into a new area. Tweenagers have learned to imagine, reason and question.

What can parents do to help their children through this whirling time of fantasy and daydreams? First and foremost, when your child announces an incredible, unrealistic goal, don't laugh. Or snicker. Or smirk. Or frown.

Just listen.

Often I will catch my four-year-old daughter acting out her fantasies with her dolls. She will be loudly singing and talking in her little-doll voices. If I sneak up and take a peek with one of those proud parental grins on my face, inevitably she will look at me, blush and put her toys away.

A parent's "isn't-that-cute?" expression will kill joy and imagination. So will a parent's scorn or disbelief.

So when your tweenager comes to you and announces that she would like to be an astronaut, smile and say you wish you had that opportunity when you were growing up.

If your son wants to develop microchips in Silicon Valley (and you don't even know how to turn a computer on), pat him on the shoulder and praise him for his intelligent ideas.

If your son or daughter wants to be a bartender or something else of which you don't approve, smile and say, "You have so much talent that you could do a thousand things more challenging." Discourage bad ideas by encouraging good ideas.

We asked our tweenagers what they wanted to do with their lives. Each response was truly individual and ranged from a vague "whatever God wants me to do" to "full-time Christian ministry." Mike wants to become a gourmet chef: "I love to cook. It offers a lot of money, and it requires leadership skills which I feel I have."

Encourage creativity. Most of all, don't forget to pray. The men and women of the future are built from the dreamers of today.

Think Like a Tween

What other things do tweenagers think about? Do

they worry about the bomb, or the world population explosion, or the national deficit like we adults? None of the tweens we know do. Of course they may give such issues a passing thought, but most tweenagers are far more worried about their friends, families and school.

"I worry about my friends," says Beth, "and whether they are going to heaven or hell."

A friend of ours is an eighth-grade English teacher and she requires her students to keep daily journals. A recurring theme in the journals is "I don't have any friends. I'd rather be dead." Tweenagers are not as concerned about global affairs as they are affairs of the heart.

The Age of Reason Dawns
Angie

Mental mayhem is also evidenced by the new reasoning processes which tweenagers begin to develop. Jerome Kagan, an expert on human development, writes:

> The twelve-year-old has acquired a new cognitive competence — the disposition to examine the logic and consistency of his existing beliefs. The emergence of this competence is catalyzed by experiences that confront the adolescent with phenomena and attitudes that are not easily interpreted with his existing ideology. These intrusions nudge the preadolescent to begin an analytic reexamination of his knowledge.[1]

While a seven-year-old finds it difficult to deal with hypothetical situations or situations he knows are not true, tweenagers can more easily grasp situations that they have never before considered. But such imaginings can lead to difficult mental problems.

For instance, suppose we provided children with the

following information:

    1. All three-legged elephants are red.
    2. Sue is carrying a three-legged elephant.

If we then asked "What color is Sue's elephant?" a tweenager could easily deduce the correct answer. A seven-year-old would most likely refuse to answer because three-legged elephants don't exist and no girl could carry one.

How does this reasoning affect the daily lives of tweenagers? In countless ways. Let's illustrate:

    1. God loves man.
    2. God creates little babies.
    3. Many babies are born disfigured.
    4. If God loves man, why does He create disfigured people?

Young people who have always held the first two statements as absolutely valid will be forced to examine them again in the light of the third statement and resulting question. Many tweenagers find that everything they have been taught since birth suddenly has become tentative.

Wise parents and youth leaders have insights to draw upon in their reasoning which the average tweenager does not have. For instance, we know that God does not create disfigurements from spite. We live in a fallen world and many troubles of the world are a direct or indirect result of sin. It is a wise adult who will admit that there are questions and puzzles which are beyond human understanding or reasoning.

Another situation:

    1. My parents always know what is best for me.
    2. My parents have failed me in some way.
    3. If my parents always know what is best, how can they fail me or make a mistake?

Upon examination, most tweenagers will decide that the first statement must be false. Parents do not always know what is best, the child will reason, therefore they can fail, and perhaps their next decision for me will be the wrong one.

"Why can't I date at thirteen?" a girl may ask her parents. "All my friends are dating. I'm responsible and you always tell me I am mature for my age. Don't you trust me?"

"I'm the only one at school that hasn't seen that movie," a boy may challenge. "So what if it's rated R — the people at the theater don't care if I'm under age, and I hear worse language at school every day. Why don't you want me to see *Debbie Does Dallas on Blood Beach?*"

Such reexaminations are natural. But because the very nature of such examinations threatens everything parents have been trying to teach the child since birth, many parents are threatened when such questions arise. They try to correct the child's rationale with an authoritarian response: "It's the way it is because I say so!" Such responses only reinforce the child's doubts.

Dealing With "Gray Areas"

"Gray areas" are difficult to explain. Questions which can be settled directly from the Bible are much more simple, but few tweenagers ask simple questions. Their minds constantly ask "Why not?" Whatever *your* convictions about a gray area, be sure to find a verse which supports your position and share your answers directly from the Bible. Because the world is changing, we must share the unchanging principles of God's Word.

Debbie, a single mother, recently dealt with the gray area of soap operas with her thirteen-year-old daughter Lynn. When Debbie would come in from work she'd notice that Lynn had been squarely in front of the television soap operas since school. Debbie doesn't want Lynn to watch soap operas all day, but Lynn sees nothing wrong with the afternoon entertainment she and her friends enjoy discussing in between classes the next day at school.

"Simply saying, 'Just don't watch them because I don't want you to,' won't work," says Debbie. "That wouldn't have convinced me as a kid, and it won't convince Lynn either."

Debbie searched the Scriptures and then got together with Lynn for a talk. "Lynn, I think you should be aware that everything you see or hear is stored in your subconscious mind," she began. "And the Bible has something to say about what Christians should allow before our eyes and ears." Together they read Psalm 101:2,3: "I will walk in my house with a blameless heart. I will set before my eyes no vile thing." Mother and daughter learned the principle *together,* and both have incorporated it into their lives.

You will find that setting guidelines in gray areas is much easier if you find a scriptural principle and discuss it with your questioning tween. If your practice of "seeking and explaining" becomes a regular habit, your child will grow up with the greatest gift you could give him — the ability to use the Word of God for gaining the wisdom, guidance and comfort necessary for a complete life.

Ask Me Anything

Tweenagers have a burning desire to know. One of our most successful activities we host each year is the "Ask Me Anything" night. First we have sort of a trivia contest in which the kids participate in teams. Then we have refreshments and games, and after that we get down to serious business. Our kids write down their deepest questions on slips of paper and pass them to the center where they are collected and brought to our "panel of experts."

Our panel, composed of youth leaders and their wives, seeks to answer each question honestly, fully and scripturally.

Last year we held two separate "Ask Me Anything" panels and separated the girls from the boys. I was in on the girls' session, and the questions they asked said a lot about the way they think. The girls wanted to know if anything was wrong with rock music, Christian rock music, mini-skirts and French kissing. They asked, "How do you know when a boy likes you?" and "What if your best friend finds a new best friend?" There were girls who asked about suicide, terminal illness and relationships with step-parents. The questions were endless.

We spent forty minutes answering their questions and the basket of folded papers kept refilling magically. I have the feeling we could have spent all night there and they would have still been asking thought-provoking questions.

Some of the questions were pretty revealing:

I know several people who this year are doing things they wouldn't have even dreamed of doing last year. There are people who hated rock music last year, but this year they listen to it all the time. Why do they do this?

The girl who asked this question has no doubt noticed the tremendous "maturity" surge that occurs in girls between the seventh and eighth grades. Her friends are suddenly into music and clothing styles they would never have considered only a few months before. The physical growth surge which girls experience at this age, coupled with the onset of menstruation, changes their entire perspective.

If you are skating and some boy asks you to skate with him — you want to but you aren't allowed — what do you say to him?

This girl has apparently been told by her parents that she is not to "go with" or hold hands with a boy. She is embarrassed by the parental restriction, particularly when everyone else her own age is dividing up for the "couples only" skate. She can either cop out and say she's tired and wants to sit one out, or she can break the parental rule and risk punishment, or she can tell the boy she's not allowed to couple skate.

Here we enter an area with room for controversy. There are times when we want our children to take a stand for a principle because *they* believe it. For instance, if my child were offered a marijuana joint, I would hope she would be strong enough to stand on what *she* believes and say, "I will not harm my body. I don't believe in taking drugs," rather than refusing simply because I told her to.

There are other rules and guidelines, however, which are implemented strictly because of my *parental preference.* I may prefer that my twelve-year-old daughter not hold hands with a boy at a couple skate; however, the situation is not crucial. I doubt if I could convince any twelve-year-old of a biblical principle (other than simple obedience) in support of the rule. Therefore, if I am going to ask my child to conform to such a rule simply because of my parental preference, I need to give my child an answer or some way to "save face" when confronted by her peers.

I vividly remember being the only girl in my seventh grade gym class who did not shave her legs. One day the other girls gathered around me and asked bluntly, "Why don't you shave your legs? Won't your mother let you? Are you still a baby, or what?" If only I had an answer to give! As it was, I was stricken dumb with shame and embarrassment. Fortunately, my mother went out that very afternoon and bought me a razor. She had not intended to let me shave my legs until I was fifteen, but she wisely realized the pressure I faced. Sometimes, you see, a wise parent will re-evaluate her parental preference.

Important and foundational guidelines, however, should be molded into children's lives. A wealthy boy in our youth group planned his birthday party and invited nearly the entire seventh grade of his school. One couple objected to their daughter attending the party. They knew the boy, knew the situation, and were reasonably sure the party would be relatively unsupervised and would involve questionable activities.

Their daughter pleaded and begged, however, and they finally agreed to let her go. "But if you feel uncomfortable with anything happening there," they told her, "call us and we will come and get you."

The girl had been at the party for only ten minutes when she called her parents. The music was loud and vulgar, the kissing games embarrassed her, an R-rated videocassette was playing on the television, and the chaperons were nowhere in sight. Her parents were proud that she wanted to leave, but they were disappointed because she had told the host she wasn't feeling well. Her parents wanted her to stand on her principles, but she simply wasn't strong enough yet to tell the truth and risk the displeasure of her peers.

And They Keep on Asking . . .

Do you think it is okay to like a guy who cheats?

What do you do if a guy tries to scare you into having sex, and he is a guy you like?

How tweenagers are torn between what they know is right and what they feel is wrong! Their heads know one thing; their hearts tell them another. The two girls who asked these questions obviously know what is right, but they desperately want, above all, to "hang on to the guy." The first girl hates cheating, but she hopes someone will

100

tell her cheating is a small thing and love is more important. The second girl doesn't really want sex, but she wants to keep the guy's affection and love.

We must give our tweenagers the security and affirmation they need so they will never betray their own values in order to feel loved! Teach your children to be self-assured and self-accepting.

What if friends pressure you into liking somebody and then you start to like him but he isn't all that cute?

Can someone be pressured into liking someone even if they like someone else? Should they do what their friends say or what they want to do?

What if you like someone but your friends think that person isn't very interesting? What do you say to your friends?

Here is peer pressure at work. As you can see, single-sex peer groups are more important during the tweenage years than are guy/girl relationships. Even the restless fury of love can be tamed by the peer group!

Spiritual Matters in a Tween's Mind

Yes, tweenagers have questions galore, but they are not deep, probing questions about spiritual matters or theology. In fact we have found that junior high is not the ideal place for in-depth discipleship. Gary used to place a great deal of emphasis on one-on-one discipleship, and he often met on a regular basis with certain boys while other ladies and I met with girls who wished to be discipled. During our discipleship time we would pray, study Scripture and discuss problems. While these young people were directly involved in discipleship, everything was fine. But after they left middle school and entered high school, they seemingly forgot the deep spiritual truths we so eagerly imparted. Cars, dating and athletics became more important.

Were our hours of discipleship a complete waste of time? No. Whatever they may do, those young people will still remember that we cared enough to regularly spend time with them. They know that we care about their spiritual health, and they know the Bible is the place to turn for answers.

We still disciple kids, but today when Gary picks up a tweenage kid and takes him to McDonald's for a Coke, he is more likely to be discussing sports than sanctification. Gary might ask about friends rather than life goals, and he will challenge the young person to read at least a daily Bible passage instead of memorizing a chapter.

We have learned that the tweenage years are best for building the *foundational* life skills. There is time for God to build the complete house in the high school and college years.

Tweenagers need to learn the basics. If they come from an unchurched home, they need to learn who God is, why Jesus died and how salvation is offered. We teach lessons and relate stories about the men and women of the Bible. Most important, we stress a daily devotional habit, a prayer list and Scripture memorization.

Tweenagers from Christian homes need to learn the principles involved in choosing friends, building relationships with parents and other people, making decisions and maintaining a walk in Christ.

I believe it is very important for young people from Christian homes to have an opportunity for evangelism. Too many of our churched young people are sheltered in Christian schools and so involved in church programs that they never have the opportunity to stand for Christ in the world. Many Christian school children do not even know an unsaved person.

How can you get tweenagers excited about evangelism? It's not easy, but the one thing that will get a kid excited about leading his friends to Christ is leading a friend to Christ! Once they've done it, they want everyone to go to heaven!

To be honest, kids are not very effective at door-to-door visitation unless they are visiting their friends and have a youth pastor or other adult along. The kids usually treat visitation as more of a monotonous chore than an exciting opportunity.

We've found the best way to get a kid excited about leading someone to Christ is to encourage him or her to concentrate on one or two unsaved friends. They can invite them to Sunday school or other church functions, make them feel welcome, and pray for them consistently until they make a decision for Christ. This one-on-one "friendship" evangelism is very effective with tweenagers. Once one friend is led to the Lord, you've got an excited tweenager on your hands!

Give your tweens the chance to be a witness and a testimony for the Lord. The salt of the world does no good if it is left in the salt shaker. Tweenagers need to practice standing alone in their faith. Let them practice now while a loving home is standing by to catch them if they stumble.

The tweenage years truly set the foundation for the complete mental processes of later years. During this time tweenagers learn to reason and to accept, to question and to have faith, to love and to lead. Though these months are bewildering to parents and tweenagers alike, if communication remains open and parents and leaders are willing to carefully guide the random thoughts of tweenagers, the foundation that is established will be a strong one.

9

The Troubled Tween

Gary

No wise man ever wished to be younger.
—Jonathan Swift

Occasionally you will meet a tweenager who is, by the age of eleven or twelve, already a hardened reprobate. Walter is such a young man.

From the first moment I met him, he was hostile, rude and belligerent. He lived in a rough neighborhood, and violence and hatred were a normal part of his behavior.

He came to church only because he wanted desperately to play football on our middle school team. The public school coach wouldn't allow Walter on the school team; we accepted him because we thought perhaps he would accept the gospel. Walter was in such a state we thought surely anything would help him!

It is hard to believe that a ministry to children this young could already be a "salvage" ministry. Sadly, Walter was too far gone to be helped by our program. He alternately needed and hated us; one week he would seem to be on his best behavior (which for Walter was a sullen stare instead of a belligerent remark), but the next week he would pull something so unmanageable that we would ask him not to return. Throughout his time with us, Walter consistently rejected the gospel.

After being asked to leave each week, inevitably Walter would telephone the next week and beg to come back. We would relent, he would come back, and we would once again find ourselves regretting the decision. The last Sunday I saw Walter he was disturbing the lesson in Sunday school and a worker asked him to leave the classroom. As Al, our volunteer worker, escorted Walter from the classroom, Walter pulled a knife on Al and threatened him. Al once again asked Walter not to come back.

Tweens Face a Different World

The world our tweens face is not the same world we faced in our junior high years. And they know it. Any time you say, "When I was your age . . ." a tweenager will smirk and turn aside.

My parents grew up in a different world than I did. Two generations ago, according to Urie Bronfenbrenner, "everybody in the neighborhood minded your business. If you walked on the railroad trestle, the phone would ring at your house and your parents would know what you had done before you got back home. People on the street would tell you to button your jacket, and asked why you were not in church last Sunday. Sometimes you liked it and sometimes you didn't — but at least people *cared*."[1]

I grew up in the 1960s, a time of societal upheaval, a war against poverty, accelerated technology, civil rights, prosperity, Woodstock, Vietnam, campus unrest, *Father Knows Best,* and an outpouring of drugs and mind-altering substances. I wanted to try everything, and I was convinced my parents were so "out of it" that they couldn't possibly understand all that life made available to me.

Today's adolescent faces all of the above and more. In his world he is bombarded by the media, threatened by nuclear annihilation, encouraged to be sexually irresponsible, and allowed unprecedented freedom from adult supervision.

Sex is the message, the medium and the purported meaning of life. "The pill," says Norman Geisler, professor at Dallas Theological Seminary, "said, 'You can do it safely.' The bomb said, 'You had better do it now because you might not be alive tomorrow.' AIDS is saying 'You'd better not do it because it might kill you.'" School-based clinics which distribute condoms to students are saying: "We know you're going to do it, so just do it safely and responsibly."[2]

The unchangeable standards of my childhood—the home, a moral society, the security of a masculine father and a protective, nurturing mother—no longer exist to support today's young people.

Society May Be Killing Our Tweens

How threatening are these changes in society? Very. The only age group in our society with an *increasing* death rate is teenagers. Death rates from disease among young people have dropped dramatically, but death rates due to individual behavior have increased. From 1960 to 1980 motor vehicle deaths increased 42 percent. Suicide among the young during that same time period increased 139 percent. Homicide—young people killing other young people—increased 232 percent.[3]

Today's young people are silently crying out for help. They need to know that they have great worth, that they can find a purpose in life, and that Mom, Dad, and others really care about them. Professor Urie Bronfenbrenner has studied child development for years. As a world authority, he knows what tweenagers need: "I see in my studies of children one essential prerequisite for healthy human development and that is *someone* has to be crazy about the kid."[4]

Tweens and Suicide

A few years ago an outstanding high school junior was killed in a car accident. The community and the family mourned, but no one seemed to give more than perfunctory attention to the boy's younger brother, then fourteen.

Time passed. The younger boy began sitting alone in the cemetery next to his brother's grave. He moved into his brother's bedroom and literally tried to assume the older brother's role. His youth pastor was unaware of these happenings — he only thought the boy was shy or withdrawn.

The parents were bewildered but simply thought, "He'll grow out of it. He's only trying to cope in the best way he knows how."

On the two-year anniversary of the older brother's death, the younger brother donned his brother's varsity jacket and started up the car in the family garage. He was found dead the next morning.

Teenage suicide is not as extreme as you may think. Virtually all tweenagers, whether or not they would act upon their thoughts, *do* think about killing themselves at some time. Christian young people are as prone to this temptation as are non-Christian young people.

The other night our middle school service featured testimonies from the group. Anyone who wished to come up and address the group could. At first no one would budge and there was a general uneasiness and shuffling throughout the room. Finally one girl stood up and began to share what Christ and friends had meant in her life.

We hadn't intended it to work this way, but suddenly the theme of the evening became suicide. One boy stood up and shared that he had found his best friend dead after suicide. Another girl explained that she had attempted suicide and failed. Several kids shared that they had seriously considered suicide, but their friends had managed to talk them out of it.

The other youth leaders and I were amazed. Suicide, or attempts of suicide, seemed to be almost a fad: "If life gets too rough and you'd like to get back at your family or your friends who have hurt you, kill yourself." Somehow our tweenagers had picked up this message, and the thing which stopped them from destroying themselves was *their friends*.

One of our leaders stood and shared that Jesus could be there even when friends couldn't, but Angie and I learned something important that night: To our tweenagers, having Jesus wasn't as important as having a living, breathing, caring friend nearby. That may sound blasphemous, but it accurately reflects the way tweenagers think. They are extremely friend-oriented, and there is no one more miserable than a tweenager with no friends.

Parents, in their own way, can be friends with their tweens. Though they certainly will never replace the need for peer friendships, parents are very important to tweenagers. Dr. R. John Kinkel, who reported to the American Psychiatric Association that nearly eight of 100 U.S. teenagers attempted suicide within the past year, says that young people who have a "solid, quality relationship" with their parents are not as likely to attempt suicide as those who "have weekly blowups with their parents."[5]

Parents, he says, should watch if their adolescent

child shows signs of extreme pessimism with "an unnatural tendency to look for doomsday." Teenagers who indicate that it is unlikely they will remain married to one person or ever have children are suicidally pessimistic.[6]

Washington, D.C., psychiatrist Willie Hamlin says parents who provide little personal attention contribute to teenage suicide: "Parents sometimes are so busy working hard to provide the material things that they've neglected what the child really needs and wants—time, attention, love, and affection. The child acts out with suicide attempts to get attention."[7]

Why Suicide?

Why do tweenagers, with their "insignificant" problems of friends and loneliness, resort to such a drastic action as suicide? Fran Arrick, in *Tunnel Vision,* explains how young people think:

> Tunnel vision is the inability to see anything else in life but the loneliness and pain of that particular moment. It's the inability to step back and know that things will get better. Grown-ups know that you get over certain disappointments and setbacks, that they won't affect the rest of your life. But kids think, "I wasn't invited to a party," or "I'm breaking up with my boyfriend," and they can't see beyond that.[8]

One teenager put it this way: "It sounds crazy, but I think it's true—kids end up committing suicide to get out of their finals."[9]

Psychologist Iris Bolton of The Link Counseling Center in Atlanta feels that there are four things parents and teachers should teach their children in order to combat "tunnel vision":

> We've got to develop an individual's self-es-

teem so that each person has an internalized, intrinsic value because of who he or she is, not because of what he or she does. We've got to teach communication skills so that each person can learn to express and discuss their feelings. And we've got to teach what I call "positive failure." In a culture that promotes being "number one" in all that we do, it's important for kids to know that the effort is positive, that they can enjoy and grow from what they do regardless of the outcome. And finally we've got to help individuals learn how to handle grief. Many suicides are triggered by some sort of loss—a parent, a good grade, even a date—we've got to help people learn how to deal with losses and even grow from them.[10]

Helping a Troubled Tween

How can you help a troubled and possibly suicidal tweenager?

Be alert to the warning signs. Suicide threats, personality changes, depression, drop in school performance, themes of death in music, artwork, or school compositions, loss of friends, drug and/or alcohol abuse, and giving away prized possessions are all signs of a troubled person.

Talk to the tweenager. Let him know you're concerned about his well-being and the changes you've seen in him. Offer to pray with and/or for him. Don't be drawn into a debate about whether suicide is right or wrong.

Don't beat around the bush. Ask him directly if he has a suicide plan and try to get the how, when, where and why.

Don't act shocked at what the tweenager will tell you. If there is an underlying reason why the tweenager is trying to escape life (i.e., incest, rape, abuse), report the incident to the proper authorities.

Refer the tweenager to a professional for help. Call

111

the pastor, a counselor, the parents, a psychologist.

Remove any potential weapons from the house. Don't leave a tweenager alone if you believe the threat of suicide is immediate.

NEVER assume the tweenager is "only bluffing."

The tragedy of tweenage suicide hits fifteen families every day, and Christian families are not immune. Last week a Christian school student in our town killed himself, and this week another boy attempted to imitate the act. It is not only older teenagers who are killing themselves — at least three percent of all reported suicides between the ages of ten and twenty-four were between the ages of ten and fourteen.[11]

The need for parents and other adults to be loving friends to tweenagers has never been greater. We cannot ignore them — the cost is too great.

10

How to Make a Tweenager Your Friend

Gary

By friendship you mean the greatest love, the greatest usefulness, the most open communication, the noblest sufferings, the severest truth, the heartiest counsel, and the greatest union of minds of which brave men and women are capable.

—Jeremy Taylor

It is a pity that most young people think adults are incapable of understanding, and most adults think young people are foolish and trivial. "The conversation of the old and the young," said Samuel Johnson, "ends generally with contempt or pity on either side."

You cannot have an influence for good in a young person's life unless you have his respect. You cannot direct and mold his life until you have his friendship.

How can you cross the cultural and social "generation gap" to reach a tweenager? Must you dress like them, think like them and give up a measure of your hard-won maturity in order to relate to them?

No. In fact, adults who try to act or dress like kids usually earn only contempt. Young people want to see adults who act like adults. They want to see a hero, someone they can strive to be like. Tweens need the assurance that it is possible to grow up and be happy and well-adjusted.

It Starts With Involvement

So how do you reach tweenagers—yours or someone else's? First of all, you must be seen by kids. You must be available. This is a foundational requirement for anyone who truly wishes to positively touch the lives of young people.

Go to their activities consistently; attend the school's athletic events and band concerts. Introduce yourself to the principal of the school and meet your kids' favorite (and least favorite!) teachers. When your kids are ranting and raving about Mr. Miller the science teacher, you should know who Mr. Miller is.

What does this accomplish? The kids learn to recognize your face—they know who you are. If you work with tweenagers at church, for instance, showing up at a school event will pleasantly surprise them and show them that your commitment to them is more than a once-a-week exercise. They know an adult is not likely to attend a school function unless he or she really cares.

Parents, although Johnny or Jenny may blush to see you bragging about them, and though they probably won't want to walk into the school with you, your children will be glad to know you are there for their activities. I've heard so many adults with unhappy childhoods say, "There was never anyone there for me. No one cared enough."

Always be there when they need you, but youth workers, take care to be used, not abused. I had always taken pride in my availability, but when some of the girls from church began to call me for a ride to the mall so they could walk around for an hour or two, I realized I had become a glorified taxi service.

The telephone can also be abused. Tweenage girls love to talk and share their secrets, and if they can't get in touch with their best friends, they'll call anyone who will listen to them. Many girls, lonely for someone to talk to, began to call me and talk for an hour or two each night. I didn't mind at first, but when I realized how my wife resented the way those phone calls cut into our family time together, I stopped the phone calls. "If it is an emergency or if you need to ask a simple question, fine—call me," I told my kids. "But if you just want to talk, please come by and see me at the office or call me there." I let them know I was available *if they really needed me*. I'll never have an unlisted phone number, but I guard my family time at home by limiting my availability.

If you are a lay worker, with a family and a career of your own, you can't be available to attend every function of your city's middle school, of course. But if you can be faithful to your church's middle school activities and be willing to spend some telephone time with a tweenager who needs it, you'll be providing an invaluable service.

And parents, never limit your availability to your children. I know of exceptionally successful men who spend hours working in high-powered offices whose doors are always open to their children. Your child needs to know that you are always there and are willing to hear what they have to say.

Become a Part of the Middle School World

I realize not every lay person or parent can do *all* of the things which I am suggesting, but youth pastors, perhaps you should consider becoming a part of the middle school world. One year I concentrated my efforts on Linkhorne Middle School, a public school in our town, and was permitted to help the football coach with the team. I was strictly a volunteer (any coach can use an extra pair of hands) and soon I had many regular responsibilities. The boys on the team grew to know and trust me, and even those who had never attended our church found out that I was "OK."

Coaching Little League was another inroad to the youth of our city. I chose to coach in the minor league (ten-to twelve-year-olds) and soon found that all my areas of involvement were overlapping—Little League boys showed up in football practice at Linkhorne and eventually turned up in our Sunday school class.

In all areas, I tried to maintain a strong Christian testimony. I often counseled the boys privately. I was delighted when the head coach began to send boys to me: "This boy is starting to get into drugs, I'm afraid. Gary, you have a talk with him."

It wasn't long before I was helping coach tennis, track and basketball at the public school. The school teachers and coaches were glad for the extra help; I was thrilled that I was meeting so many new kids. Slowly and surely I was becoming a regular fixture in the world of those middle school kids.

Perhaps the most meaningful plaque I've ever received was presented to me at the close of the school year. On "Fun Day," when the school held their awards ceremony, I was presented with two plaques for my help. When I saw the glowing faces of the boys I had helped and worked with, I knew the long hours under a hot sun were all worthwhile.

Parents, when your child registers at the area middle school, make an appointment with the principal and let him know you are concerned about your child. Attend PTA meetings. Schedule conferences with your child's teachers when there is *not* a problem with his grades or his attitude.

Get out there and be known! Don't sit in your little church "bubble," isolated and insulated from the world. The world of tweenage kids is often shocking, irreverent and perhaps not the antiseptic Christian world you enjoy. But you will never be more than a glorified chaperon or an uninformed parent unless you are willing to get out there and get involved for the sake of kids. Never miss an opportunity to expand your base of contacts.

After kids see you around and they learn who and what you are, many will come to talk and "check you out." Here is where a sense of humor comes in handy. Let kids know you are fun and have fun with them! Be relaxed and be yourself. As you get to know kids, those who need someone special may seek you out and you can counsel them and invite them to church.

What Tweens Need From You

And what do tweenagers want from their parents and other adults? Elizabeth, a tweenager, says that she wants a relationship "where my parents can believe me and trust me. Without trust I wouldn't have any privileges. I love my parents, and I want to keep it that way."

Michael says, "I want my parents to give me freedom and to understand me." A tall order, isn't it?

The Friendship Factor

Jim Zug is a Christian science teacher in a public

middle school. He's popular, yet firm, and several kids hang around his classroom after school. Why? Because he is their friend.

Jim's "secrets" are simple: "I get to know their names quickly. They know that you really know who they are if you simply remember their name. When I'm with them I talk *to* them, not *at* them. When we talk, we don't talk about school or science or the latest exam. We talk about things they care about."

Greg Wheeler is another popular teacher. "I try to be a friend to them and keep their respect," he says. "I find out what they're interested in and always ask about it: 'How did you do in your game last week?' Kids like to talk about *their* activities, not yours."

Jane Randlett, a lay worker, a terrific mother, and the mother of a tweenager, believes it is important for the friendship between child and parent to begin in the childhood years: "It involves doing what they want to do and spending time in their activities. The friendship involves listening, having fun and being together."

When you take your child out to spend time with him, do you drag him to your adult activities or do you let your child choose the activity? Tom, a busy father with a demanding job, always prided himself on the hours he and his son spent together. The twelve-year-old son, however, recently began to pull away from his father—he doesn't want to be with Tom. Why? Because Tom had taken him to adult meetings, adult games, adult events. The boy had never been a participant in their time together; he had only been a token tribute to Tom's fatherhood.

Sharing Christ With Your Tween

After you have established a friendship and you have taken the time to really know that tweenager, share

Christ with him. Sharing the gospel *before* you have taken the time to get to know a tween may turn him off. "Preaching" at kids doesn't show you care; it implies that you are speaking out of obligation. Why should a tweenager trust that what you are offering is right for him if you haven't taken the time to get to know him or his problems? Sharing the gospel with a kid who is your friend shows that you care enough to discern his needs and provide the right answer.

When you have been seen by kids and known by kids, it follows that you will be understood by kids. When tweens understand you and what you are about, and when they can trust you and know that you honestly want to help them, then they will be willing to accept the gospel you present. Kids have no problem realizing they sin—they have clear-cut ideas of what is right and wrong. But due to the negative self-image which many possess, they may have a problem believing that Christ loves them enough to die for them. But if a tweenager can look at you and see God loving him through you, he can believe.

Making Contacts With Non-Christian Kids

How can you contact non-Christian kids? First, get your Christian tweenagers to bring their unsaved friends to church activities, Sunday school, or by your office or home for a visit. One of my dedicated Christian boys, Tommy, was concerned about his friend, Steve. "You bring Steve by my office," I told him. "We'll have a couple of Cokes and I'll talk to him." Tommy assured Steve that I was "OK," and they stopped by. After spending some time in idle chatter and getting to know one another, I was able to share the gospel with Steve.

You can also contact kids casually by playing sports or other recreational activities. Our YMCA has "open gym" each afternoon and during the summer I try to play basketball every day. I meet many new adults from the community and many teenagers down on the basketball court. We learn respect for each other on the playing field, and once again I've made new contacts.

Church-sponsored activities are also great for making contacts. Once each year our church invites all junior and senior high students to "join us on the bus" as we travel to Kings' Dominion, an amusement park three hours away. Kids come by the thousands and we let them spend all day in the park. After a day of fun and freedom, they meet on the bus to go home, and we present a short gospel message. Many kids accept the Lord on the bus.

Other effective contacts include home visitation, phone calls "just to say hello," and written contacts. Our Sunday school department routinely sends a birthday card to each member, and I've found that kids love receiving a note in the mail. My notes are always short, but whether I simply ask, "How are you doing?" or tell them that I have been praying for them, kids always let me know how much they appreciate my letters. Nothing encourages a tweenager more than an adult's letter saying "thanks" for something nice they have done for someone or complimenting them on their kindness, courtesy, concern, spiritual growth or consistency.

It is helpful for youth leaders to write to parents, too. In today's society, when sexual perverts lure children in hundreds of neighborhoods and gun-toting snipers lurk in parking lots, I understand why many parents initially mistrust me. You see, tweenagers go home and talk about admired adults, and many parents do not know what to make of the influence of a youth pastor. I've found it is important to meet parents, explain that I am trying to help their child grow spiritually, and that I will never attempt to undermine their parental authority. I've met parents, Christian and non-Christian, who could care less about where their children are going or with whom. I've also met parents who truly resented any outsider's influence on their child. Then again, I've met parents who are thrilled beyond measure that someone cares enough to listen to their child.

We have seen success stories of tweenagers who accepted the Lord and eventually led their entire families to receive the gospel and become part of a church. Those testimonies, and the record of answered prayers in my prayer journal, keep us going.

Do You Remember When You Were Thirteen?

I suppose I have a special concern for very young teenagers because I remember myself in junior high — skinny, high-voiced, sensitive, shy and terribly insecure.

I remember my eighth-grade Christmas choir concert. I had been chosen to step out between songs and announce the name of the next number. I was nervous, but more than that, I was profoundly embarrassed because hundreds of eyes would be centered on me and me alone. After the opening song, those eyes turned to me. I stepped out on cue, took a deep breath, and fainted. Whack! My chin hit the edge of the risers and I carry the physical scar to this day.

My wife and I laugh over that story today, but deep inside I still remember how it felt to be awkward and embarrassed. Other tweenagers have those same feelings, and they need to hear words of affirmation, love and encouragement. I want them to have someone to look toward for support, friendship and emotional and spiritual leadership. That is why I am a junior high youth pastor.

Too many times I have met bitter, broken and confused students in senior high school who carry battle scars from junior high. Many are caught in a web of apathy, never having resolved those crucial questions of self-worth and identity. Men and women who work with senior highers often spend hours simply trying to salvage spirits broken in junior high school when they ought to be preparing teenagers for the threshold of adulthood.

When tweenage ministry is well done, it is an invisible investment, a firm foundation which cannot be shaken through the ensuing years.

Tweens Do Grow Up!

I've been pastoring tweenagers for twelve years now, and the scrawny kids I first met as sixth graders are now married and rearing children of their own. Earlier I shared with you letters from giggly tweenage girls. Believe it or not, those girls grew up. The giddy giggles are gone, but the friendship remains.

> Dear Gary:
> Please don't think I've forgotten about you. You are still a very important person to me. I'm very thankful to God for allowing us to become close—you are truly a blessing sent from heaven. Thanks for caring.
> Cindy, age twenty

> Dear Gary:
> I know it's been a long time since I've written or talked to you! It was good to see and talk to you yesterday—it wasn't much, but it meant a lot to me! I still feel as close to you as I have always been, because you always promised me you would be there and that's great to hear! You have done so much for me I'll never forget it! Thank you for helping me along the way in junior high! Have a super day!
> Teresa, age nineteen

122

Anyone who simply loves and befriends a tweenager could get similar letters. Tweens are unique people, worth the time it takes to understand their special needs and insecurities. After all, they're the adults of tomorrow.

The Toughest Job You'll Ever Love

We're the first to admit that tweens can be a difficult age group to work with. But *someone* has to be willing to risk some personal comfort. Tweenagers don't care how old you are or whose parent you are—they simply need someone who cares enough to be consistent.

What special qualities does it take to work with tweenagers? Patience, a lot of love, a sense of humor, honesty and the ability to never be (or act) shocked.

It is also important to be transparent with middle schoolers. If you have a hidden agenda or a subconscious reason for working with them, they'll discern it in no time. If you think taking your kid to a football game will get you a "Father of the Year" nomination, or if you're trying to win points with you pastor by volunteering in the youth department, no tweenager will take you seriously.

Middle schoolers aren't children any more. They've learned enough about the adult world to recognize hypocrisy, and they're blunt enough to point it out.

If you're making a token effort to be with tweenagers

- to impress another adult
- to ease a guilty conscience
- to fulfill a hastily-made promise
- to tag along with your spouse
- to keep an eye on your kid
- or to give an impression of being "young and crazy"

you've got the wrong motivation.

The only correct motivation for being with tweenagers is love. They only want—and desperately need—someone to love them through this crazy stage of adolescent development.

As you organize your life this week, think about the tweenager you love. How can you change your love into an action? By recognizing what is urgent and what is important:

Urgent things demand instant action.

Important things require careful attention.

Urgent things clamor loudly.

Important things are most often quiet and unobtrusive.

Urgent things are many.

Important things are few.

Urgent things are resolved and soon forgotten.

Important things, though eternal, are often neglected.

What is urgent? A report demanded by your boss; a meeting with big-name people; a reckless drive through traffic to catch a flight.

What is important? The time you spend with your family, laughing, loving and sharing; the time you spend with God and in prayer; the time you spend one-on-one with a tweenager who needs you.

Remind your tween that he is precious to you and to God.

Teach him that life is full of joys and sorrows, but that God always brings us through the difficult times stronger than we were before.

Respect his growing independence and allow a

measure of privacy.

Instruct him by assessing fairly his requests for privileges and responsibilities.

Most important of all, love him by being there when he needs you . . . with an open ear and a receptive heart.

NOTES

CHAPTER ONE
1. Thomas J. Cottle, "The Connections of Adolescence," *12 to 16: Early Adolescence* (New York: W. W. Norton & Company, 1972), p. 299.
2. Edward C. Martin, "The Early Adolescent in School," *12 to 16: Early Adolescence* (New York: W. W. Norton & Company, 1972), p. 181.
3. Martin, "The Early Adolescent," p. 182.

CHAPTER TWO
1. Jerome Kagan, "A Conception of Early Adolescence," *12 to 16: Early Adolescence* (New York: W. W. Norton & Company, 1972), p. 100.
2. Adapted from Bruce B. Barton, "Identity Crisis in Teenagers," *Parents and Teenagers* (Wheaton, IL: Victor Books, 1984), p. 158. Used by permission.
3. Personal interview with Clyde Narramore, April 28, 1986.

CHAPTER THREE
1. James Dobson, "The Most Difficult Period of Adolescence," *Parents and Teenagers* (Wheaton, IL: Victor Books, 1984), p. 157.
2. Chad Gordon, "Social Characteristics," *12 to 16: Early Adolescence* (New York: W. W. Norton & Company, 1972), p. 39.
3. Edward C. Martin, "The Early Adolescent in School," *12 to 16: Early Adolescence* (New York: W. W. Norton & Company, 1972), p. 190.
4. Urie Bronfenbrenner, *The Ecology of Human Development* (Cambridge: Harvard University Press, 1979), p. 284.
5. Urie Bronfenbrenner as quoted by John Janeway Conger in "A World They Never Knew," *12 to 16: Early Adolescence* (New York: W. W. Norton & Company, 1972), p. 221.
6. Martin, "The Early Adolescent," p. 192.
7. John Janeway Conger, "A World They Never Knew," *12 to 16: Early Adolescence* (New York: W. W. Norton & Company, 1972), p. 221.
8. William Bennett, a speech given at Liberty University, Lynchburg, Virginia, April 23, 1986.
9. *Children and Parents: Together in the World,* Report of Forum 15, 1970 White House Conference on Children (Washington, D.C.: Superintendent of Documents, 1971).

CHAPTER FOUR
1. James Dobson, "Why Teens Don't Like to Be Seen with Their Parents," *Parents and Teenagers* (Wheaton, IL: Victor Books, 1984), p. 195.
2. Gregory Monaco, "Your Teen Wouldn't Swear, Would He?" *Parents and Teenagers* (Wheaton, IL: Victor Books, 1984), p. 190.
3. Lawrence Kohlberg and Carol Gilligan, "The Adolescent as a Philosopher," *12 to 16: Early Adolescence* (New York: W. W. Norton & Company, 1972), p. 153.
4. Personal interview with Surgeon General Koop, January 18, 1987.
5. "The Only Thing Wasted Is You" (Silver Spring, MD: National Federation of Parents for a Drug-Free Youth).
6. Adapted from "Hey Girls--Look What Alcohol Can Do For You" (Silver Spring, MD: National Federation of Parents for a Drug-Free Youth).

CHAPTER FIVE
1. Thomas J. Cottle, "The Connections of Adolescence," *12 to 16: Early Adolescence* (New York: W. W. Norton & Company, 1972), p. 296.

2. Cottle, "The Connections of Adolescence," p. 296.

CHAPTER SIX
1. Grace Ketterman, M.D., "Positive Rebellion," *Parents and Teenagers* (Wheaton, IL: Victor Books, 1984), pp. 485-86.
2. Arthur L. Stitchcombe, *Rebellion in a High School* (Chicago: Quadrangle Books, 1964), referred to by David Bakan in "Adolescence in America," *12 to 16: Early Adolescence* (New York: W. W. Norton & Company, 1972), p. 84.
3. Adapted from James Dobson, *Dr. Dobson Answers Your Questions* (Wheaton, IL: Tyndale House, 1987), pp. 270-72.

CHAPTER SEVEN
1. James Dobson, "Your Teens are Growing Up Faster Than You Did," *Parents and Teenagers* (Wheaton, IL: Victor Books, 1984), p. 176.
2. Grace Ketterman, M.D., "Why Girls Mature Faster Than Boys," *Parents and Teenagers* (Wheaton, IL: Victor Books, 1984), p. 178.
3. Clifford and Joyce Penner, *A Gift for All Ages* (Waco, TX: Word Books, 1986), pp. 105-06.
4. Personal interview with Surgeon General Koop, January 18, 1987.
5. Personal interview with Norman Geisler, March 16, 1987.
6. Judy Blume, "What Your Kids Wish They Could Tell You," *Family Circle* (November 11, 1986), pp. 18ff. Used by permission of the Putnam Publishing Group.
7. J. M. Tanner, "Sequence, Tempo, and Individual Variation," *12 to 16: Early Adolescence* (New York: W. W. Norton & Company, 1972), p. 19.
8. Paul D. Meier, *Christian Child-Rearing and Personality Development* (Grand Rapids, MI: Baker Book House, 1977), p. 180.

CHAPTER EIGHT
1. Jerome Kagan, "A Conception of Early Adolescence," *12 to 16: Early Adolescence* (New York: W. W. Norton & Company, 1972), p. 93.

CHAPTER NINE
1. John Janeway Conger, "A World They Never Knew," *12 to 16: Early Adolescence* (New York: W. W. Norton & Company, 1972), p. 199.
2. Personal interview with Norman Geisler, March 16, 1987.
3. William Bennett, a speech given at Liberty University, Lynchburg, Virginia, April 23, 1986.
4. Urie Brofenbrenner as quoted by William Bennett, a speech given at Liberty University, April 23, 1986.
5. "Teen Suicide Rate Soars Even Higher," *Focus on the Family* (July 1986), p. 4.
6. "Teen Suicide Rate," p. 4.
7. Jeannye Thornton, "Behind a Surge in Suicides of Young People," *U.S. News and World Report* (June 20, 1983), p. 66.
8. Mary Ann O'Roark, "The Alarming Rise in Teenage Suicide," *McCall's* (January 1982), p. 16.
9. O'Roark, "The Alarming Rise," p. 22.
10. O'Roark, "The Alarming Rise," p. 120.
11. "What Predicts Adolescent Suicide?" *Essentials of Adolescence* (Volume 9, No. 4, 1983), p. 1.